MW00612134

Oral History
Projects
in Your
Classroom

Linda P. Wood

ORAL HISTORY

ASSOCIATION

About the Oral History Association

The Oral History Association is a society of scholars, students, local historians, and others concerned with the application of professional standards to the collection, preservation, dissemination, and use of oral testimony. It serves as a bridge between scholars of various disciplines and also between these scholars and librarians, archivists, teachers, journalists, authors, and others engaged in recording personal and institutional histories. Members of the Oral History Association exchange views and learn of new developments through the annual meeting, a quarterly newsletter, *Oral History Review,* and our pamphlet series. Our pamphlets offer basic and useful information about many aspects of conducting, interpreting, processing, and publishing oral history interviews, and managing oral history programs and projects. For more information about membership in the Oral History Association, and to order copies of this workbook and other pamphlets in the series, please contact the Oral History Association at Dickinson College, P.O. Box 1773, Carlisle, PA 17013-2896. E-mail us at oha@dickinson.edu, and visit our website at www.dickinson.edu/oha.

About the Author

Linda P. Wood was a library media specialist at South Kingstown High School in Wakefield, Rhode Island, for over 20 years. During those years, she conducted several student based oral history projects in collaboration with classroom teachers.

Companion video

History from the Living: The Organization and Craft of Oral History, based on "1968: The Whole World Was Watching" oral history project, South Kingstown High School, Wakefield, RI. Newport, RI: Grin Productions, 1998. Running time 17 minutes 14 seconds. Available from J. Long, Grin Productions, 6 Carey Street, Newport, RI 02804, $20.

©2001 by the Oral History Association. All rights reserved

Printed in the United States of America

Foreword by Barry A. Lanman   1

Preface *Description of Five Classroom Projects*   2

Introduction by Marjorie L. McLellan   5

Chapter 1 *Getting Started*   10

  ■ Using Oral History in the Classroom   10

  ■ Oral History and the Local Scene   12

  ■ Creating a Model Portfolio   13

Chapter 2 *Developing an Oral History Project*   15

  ■ Classroom Curriculum   16

  ■ Administrative and Community Support   20

  ■ The Character and Resources of the Community   22

  ■ Funding   23

  ■ Focus for the Project   25

  ■ Scope and Length of the Project   27

Chapter 3 *The Oral History Project*   31

  ■ Developing a Knowledge Base   31

  ■ Identifying Narrators   33

  ■ Research Ethics   35

  ■ Interview Questions   37

  ■ The Practice Interview   38

  ■ Equipment for the Project   39

  ■ The Interview   42

  ■ The Interview Index   43

  ■ Keeping Track of All the Parts   43

CONTENTS

Chapter 4 *After the Interview*   45

   ■ In the Classroom   45

   ■ Transcribing the Interview   46

   ■ Assignments   49

   ■ Public Programs   51

   ■ Preserving the Historical Documents   53

   ■ Assessment and Student Evaluation   53

Conclusion   55

Bibliography   56

Handouts and Reproducible Forms   59

   1   Interviews and Transcripts as Primary Sources   61

   2   Witness to History   63

   3   Narrator Information Form   65

   4   Letter to Potential Narrator   67

   5   Making Contact with the Narrator   69

   6   Receipt for Borrowed Documents   71

   7   Legal Release Form   73

   8   Types of Questions to Ask   75

   9   Tips on How to Interview   77

   10   "Invented" Interviews for Practice   79

   11   Information Kit; Checklist for the Interview   81

   12   Keeping Track of the Parts   83

   13   Student Survey Evaluation   85

   14   Project Evaluation Form   87

Oral history classroom projects exist, indeed flourish, in every part of the United States, exploring their own local communities and offering students the rare opportunity to become involved with their subject matter in an interactive process of learning. Some teachers use oral history to teach specific course content, such as the Depression or World War II. Others use it to develop interpersonal and social skills, as students go out into the community and interview adults. Still others focus on affective education, as students explore the feelings and conflicts experienced by others . . .. Some projects are large and well known, such as the *Foxfire* program, while many others operate in relative obscurity, little known outside their own school and community. Some enjoy substantial financial support while others exist on a meager budget. However, all have a talented and interested teacher, not content with the status quo, who with imagination and determination has created a new approach to learning for students.

Barry Lanman

Dr. Barry A. Lanman, Baltimore County Public Schools, Baltimore, MD, has served as the chair of the Oral History Association's Education Committee.

Perspectives of Teachers and Students

Students are learning how to listen, communicate, write and spell, while learning more about their own history and heritage.

Sherry Spitler
Program Director of The Tamiisix Project: Teaching Cultural Heritage and Skills Through Oral History, Aleutian Region School District, The Aleutian Islands, AK

I have found that community history breaks down student indifference. It helps students understand their neighborhood and themselves and gives new meaning to the term "roots".

Howard J. Shorr
The Boye Heights Project, Theodore Roosevelt High School, Los Angeles, CA

Oral history has been an important part of my teaching program for the past seven years. Although initially I viewed it only as a method to collect a local history of the Depression, I have since become impressed by the versatility and the effectiveness of this research tool. Students, armed with tape recorders and a genuine desire to learn, have gathered insights into the past that are colored by the laughter and tears of the participants. Their view of

history has been enriched by seeing textbook facts through the eyes of an individual who has experienced the event.

Patricia Grimmer
Carbondale Community High School, Carbondale, IL

It helped me understand the human causes, not just 'the war began because' . . . but why it began, who was involved and most importantly—how they felt.

Richard Hankin
student

Oral history helps children see the continuity of life . . . It teaches the similarities in people of different generations and breaks down stereotypes, especially between generations.

Nancy Topp
Elk Grove Village School, Elk Grove Village, IL

Oral history is learning by doing.

Kelly McConville
student

Excerpted from Oral History in the Secondary School Classroom *by Barry A. Lanman and George L. Mehaffy (Oral History Association Pamphlet Series, 1988)*

Description of Five Classroom Projects

In this guide, sample forms, handouts, numerous examples, curriculum suggestions, and discussion questions are taken directly from real-life classroom oral history projects around the country. The five classroom projects described below serve as core models which can be adapted to the teacher's own classroom situations. These projects were directed by Wood in collaboration with language arts and social studies teachers, and were funded in part by the Rhode Island Committee for the Humanities.

❶ *Yankee Ingenuity: Can the Government It Forged Survive?*
A nine-week unit for seniors in an after-school independent study program. The three towns in the regional school district have a town meeting form of government. One of the rural communities was the proposed site for construction of a nuclear power plant. Twelve students interviewed "yankees," life-long residents who were over 65 years old, and whose parents and grandparents had lived in the community. The purpose was to learn how the local government could address the national issues raised by the proposed nuclear power plant construction. The students' questions dealt with family, education, town government, and the power plant. The students' findings were presented at public forums held in each community's town hall. A compilation of the transcripts of the interviews was made available at the meetings and placed in local libraries. The students, assisted by a historian and a political scientist from the state university, researched and prepared the interview questions, conducted the interviews, and participated in the public forums.

❷ *In the Wake of '38*
A semester project in an English class focused on the events of September 21, 1938, when a devastating hurricane hit Rhode Island, with a strength and power never before or since equaled. Fifteen ninth to eleventh grade students participated in the oral history project. Research included eyewitness accounts in state newspapers, diaries, letters, and photographs collected from narrators and from the archives of local and state historical societies. A scholar from the university helped the students focus their research, prepare the interview questions, and helped them to interpret the narrators' responses. The students prepared a slide/tape program using tape-recorded voices and photographs donated by the narrators. Bound transcripts of the interviews were distributed at several public events, which included a guided

walk on a beach where 40 homes were wiped away by the hurricane. A public forum was held that asked the question, "What should Rhode Islanders have learned from the Hurricane of '38?", which provoked lively discussion among the students, narrators, members of the local community, and invited state government officials.

❸ *"What Did You Do In the War, Garndma?"*

For this semester-long project in a ninth grade English class, students read novels, plays and poetry about the war, including *The Good War* by Studs Terkel, editor and compiler of many popular books utilizing oral histories. Each student interviewed two women, selected for their roles during the war. Again, professors from the university helped the students conduct research, prepare interview questions, select narrators, and critique the interviews. Students wrote the narrators' stories from the interview transcripts. The professors and teachers helped each student focus on the historically significant aspects of each interview. The stories, augmented by photographs, pictures and memorabilia, were assembled in a publication, which included essays written by the teachers and scholars. Two public forums were held; one focused on oral history as a classroom project, the other on the narrators' experiences within the historical context. The publication has since been adapted for the Internet and can be found at http://www.stg.brown.edu/projects/WWII_Women/.

❹ *The Family in the Fifties: Hope, Fear, and Rock 'n' Roll*

Tenth grade students in an English class focused on a variety of issues that affected American families of the 1950's. They read *Catcher In the Rye,* a sampling of Beat poetry, and saw several film and television clips. Each student then interviewed two persons, selected to represent a variety of roles and issues of the 1950's, such as women's rights, the Cold War, civil liberties, and popular culture. Two scholars worked with the students to keep them focused on the issues and to help them write about historically significant aspects of the decade. The students wrote the narrators' stories based on the transcripts of their interviews. A publication of the stories and essays was distributed by the state historical society through the public libraries. A public forum focusing on popular culture was held at the historical society on the birthday of Elvis Presley at which an Elvis impersonator entertained the attendees. A second public forum concerning civil liberties was held on the anniversary of the day in 1955 when Rosa Parks refused to move from her seat in a Montgomery, Alabama, public bus.

⑤ *1968: The Whole World Was Watching*

This project focused on 1968, a single tumultuous year in a decade of turmoil. By examining one year in detail, the students were able to assemble a montage of the issues which confronted America: Civil Rights, the Vietnam War and anti-war protests, women's rights, the politics and election of 1968, and the space program. Access to new technology permitted a full integration of voice, video, photograph and print with links to primary and secondary sources to support and add depth and significance to the interviews. Professors worked with the students, the teachers, and a computer scholar to prepare an Internet site in conjunction with the printed publication. The web site can be viewed at www.stg.brown.edu/projects/1968/.

These five oral history projects have successfully captured the imaginations of students and the community, demonstrating that learning does not have to take place within the four walls of a school classroom, but can expand to the local community, to the state, and to the world. The students become the historians and their interviews become primary source materials. The final product is an historical record available to future scholars. The students learned to communicate their interpretations of historical events in print, in public forums, in video documentaries or slide programs, and on the Internet. This guide was created to assist teachers and other educators to engage students in a collaborative learning process that connects them to their own histories, their communities, and the world beyond.

History is assembled from the lives of people caught up in experiences and events. The recorded memories of these experiences are oral history. Motivating students to explore the past can be a difficult sell; oral history breathes life into the textbook narrative. In the interview, students observe narrators trying to explain and to capture the meaning and implications of their own stories. In this sense, the student and the narrator are constructing a unique document—a record of the past as remembered in the present. Students who find history to be a boring collection of facts can be turned on by direct involvement in the stories of people who were there as events occurred. Each narrator's eyewitness account adds to the mosaic as students gradually piece together a sense of historic events and the meaning of these events in people's lives. When the puzzle is complete, the students can better grasp the significance of the past from the composite voices of the narrators.

In *The Presence of the Past: Popular Uses of History in American Life,* Roy Rosenzweig and David Thelen found that history as taught in school does not inspire a strong connection to the past (1998). However, they concluded that while popular history making is alive and well, it is articulated in a different vocabulary:

> . . . *history* conjured up something done by famous people that others studied in school; respondents said history was formal, analytical, official, or distant. Words like *heritage* and *tradition* conjured up warm and fuzzy feelings but not very rich experience or sharp observation. *The past* was the term that best invited people to talk about family, race, and nation, about where they had come from and what they had learned along the way. *Trust* was the concept that best captured how people viewed sources of information about the past. And the metaphor that best captured what mattered to them in the past could be elicited by the concept of *connection*. To which pasts did they feel most connected?

Oral history projects connect students to the past by the gathering and analysis of primary source material—raw data—from those who were involved in or experienced the events. Your classroom will come alive as the recorded histories are collected by students and examined against the context of research from other primary sources, as well as secondary sources. As the mosaic takes shape, student historians will learn to interpret and make sense of the complexity of the past. Oral history is the best kind of learning because it actively engages the students, using their natural curiosity about other people to provide an emotional context too often missing from textbook lessons.

Marjorie L. McLellan

Professor McLellan is Director of the Public History Program at Wright State University in Dayton, OH, and has served as the chair of the Oral History Association's Education Committee.

In the first few moments of the labor history film *Uprising of '34* we see scenes of textile factory machinery and textile workers and we hear the workers identify themselves as "lintheads." In a steel town, hundreds of miles away and sixty years after the strike, the first moments of the film elicit provocative student comments about the ways in which these workers perceive themselves. Students ask what "linthead" signifies about the workers' experiences (Does "linthead" reflect pride or humiliation?), and comment on how they have viewed their own blue-collar families, and finally on how they view others—employers, the Japanese, and the world beyond. Students come to develop a more critical perspective as they interrogate the value and meaning of interviews as historical evidence.

Oral histories reflect a "point of view," an individual's recollection and reflection. In the excerpt from a student interview (Handout 1), Sullivan, a Democratic Party activist, recalled the 1968 convention. Students look for information subject to fact checking such as, "was there barbed wire around the convention hall?" and they discuss how to find out; however, students also speculate about his views of the familiar, clean cut, Ohio college students in contrast to the anonymous, dangerous agitators. The interview suggests the importance of story telling in Sullivan's relationship to the past, and students begin to think about how we use the past in everyday life. Through interviews we tease out subjective factors such as values, perspective, justification, regret, memory and aspirations. We learn what the narrator has learned from experience and events. Students learn that, at times, a pause or a gesture can be far more revealing than words. Oral history interviews lend themselves to careful questioning, introducing students to the problems of historical scholarship while exercising and enhancing critical thinking skills. Moving from a single interview to a variety of sources, students see developments from many different and even conflicting points of view.

Oral history gives us glimpses of society and culture in past times. Interviews have, for a long time, added a reflective and personal dimension to what we know about decision-makers and events. However, oral histories also make visible the experiences and lives of those who leave few written records, thus adding new dimensions to our knowledge and understanding of the past. Oral history can foster a lively, democratic, more inclusive, and critical understanding of the past. A class discussion leading up to an oral history project might focus, for example, on the life of civil rights activist Fannie Lou Hamer. Born to sharecroppers in Montgomery County, Mississippi, she was the youngest of twenty children. She lost her job and her home when she set out to register to vote in 1962. She testified before Congress, sheltered and advised young activists, was beaten and jailed, visited Africa with Harry Belafonte, and, as many civil rights activists interviewed later recalled, she sang and she sang. She said, "I'm tired of being tired," and as vice chair of the Mississippi Freedom Democratic Party, Hamer challenged the legitimacy of the Mississippi delegation to the 1964 Democratic National Convention and thus the party candidate, President Lyndon Baines Johnson. Hamer did not leave diaries, letters or memoirs, but she lived on in peoples' memories. Hamer's reflections and those of many who worked with her are recorded in interviews. Unita Blackwell, who served with the Mississippi Freedom Democratic Party and spoke to the Democratic National Convention twenty years later, said, "I felt tears because Fannie Lou Hamer should have been standing there. She was standing there in us . . .." Oral history's value as a record and a testimonial of, in Julian Bond's words, "the ordinary people who did extraordinary things" in the Civil Rights Movement is tangible and immediate. However, oral history offers an invaluable means to document the lives of people who have, through their labor, their everyday decisions, and their sometimes extraordinary accomplishments, built the world that we know today.

■ *Project Suggestion*

This is a model project highlighted by the Department of Education. Fifth grade students contribute to a long-term, multidisciplinary project documenting and sharing the stories of local, state, and national leaders. The central theme of the interviews is discrimination and how individuals have dealt with this obstacle in their own lives. Students research and learn about the interview process and then adapt interview guidelines for their projects. Students develop an interview outline and specific questions and practice interviewing skills. Students conduct their interviews in teams (interviewer, camera operator, and recorder). The teams review and critique their own interviews and then transcribe and summarize the recordings using the notes from the interview. They enter the text into the computer for editing and formatting Students learn about social studies, community resources, cultural organizations, the impact of discrimination, research, reading, writing and editing, public presentation, graphic arts, and technological skills. http://inet.ed.gov/pubs/EdReformStudies/EdTech/multultural.html

**The
Multicultural Heroes
Project**

*Frank Paul Elementary
School
Salinas, CA*

Oral history interviews can serve two distinct goals: to gather information about the past, and to learn about the meaning and significance of the past to the present. The first-hand narratives and recollections help students to realize that they and their families and communities are actors on the historical stage. Oral history often brings the multi-cultural, multi-ethnic nature of American society home to students. Settlement house activist Jane Addams recognized the valuable resources close at hand:

The children long that the school teacher should know something about the lives their parents lead and should be able to reprove the hooting children who make fun of the Italian mother because she wears a kerchief on her head, not only because they are rude but also because they are stupid. We send young people to Europe to see Italy, but we do not utilize Italy when it lies about the schoolhouse. If the body of teachers . . . could take hold of the immigrant colonies, could bring out of them their handicrafts and occupations, their traditions, their folk songs . . . could get the children to bring these things into the school as the material from which culture is made . . . they would discover by comparison that which they have given them now is a poor . . . and vulgar thing.

Oral history projects should not be an invitation to turn individual students and their families into representative examples of their own cultures. A teacher must reach beyond the individual child to forge connections to ethnic, religious, occupational, and other groups in the community.

Narrators give of their time, their reservoir of memories, and their trust in doing an oral history interview. The student, the teacher, and the class are, in turn, obliged to give something back—both to give courtesy and respect to the narrator and to share the knowledge that they have collected with wider publics. The latter can be accomplished through building an archives in concert with a local library or historical society, hosting a reception or ceremony, producing an exhibit, publishing a magazine, developing an Internet project, or producing a community performance. As students research and write, they become aware that they are working on a public history project with a local audience; this enhances both the quality of work and student pride in the results of their effort. Elliot Wigginton described the beginnings of the Foxfire Program at Rabun Gap High School, in Rabun Gap, Georgia:

The first interview ever conducted by my students happened in November 1966, when four of them, one evening after school, tape recorded retired sheriff Luther Rickman telling the story of the robbery of the bank of Clayton by the Zade Sprinkle gang in 1936. That interview appeared in the very first issue of *Foxfire* magazine, and even though we had intended to publish that magazine only once (moving on, then, to some other project that would also illustrate to my ninth and tenth graders the function of language arts in the real world) the community response was so immediate and so positive that students . . . have continued to produce the magazine quarterly ever since.

Foxfire is the most familiar of oral history and cultural heritage projects initiated by teachers in journalism, language arts, literature, history, economics, ethnic heritage, the arts, and other disciplines. An oral history project bridges the generations, involves young people with their elders, and enhances a school's visibility in, and engagement with, the community.

Oral history can be an effective and exciting tool for teachers from the middle school to the high school. The first chapter of this guide outlines a program of study and practice through which the teacher can learn more about oral history while introducing new concepts and perspectives to students. The second chapter discusses project planning, including institutional obstacles and ways to overcome these and to garner support and resources from administrators, the community, and the students. The third chapter gives an overview and guidelines for the oral history project itself. Chapter 4 explores what comes after the interview: how to evaluate student work, how to preserve the historical record produced, and how to share the student interviews in the both the classroom and the community. The Education Committee of the Oral History Association has gathered together examples of oral history assignments and projects from teachers, historians, and archivists—many of these projects were presented at the Association's annual meetings. Others have been gathered from the Internet. As this teaching guide makes clear, it is not just for the history or social studies teacher. English teachers, school librarians, science teachers, health and business teachers can enliven the learning experience by embracing an oral history project in their classrooms. This guide is written for *all* teachers and *all* students.

1

GETTING STARTED

Oral history is an exciting and multifaceted learning experience with opportunities for public recognition of student accomplishments. However, before you commit your students, your school, and yourself to an oral history project, think about the following questions so that you can share your enthusiasm with others later. How did you get interested in using oral history? What learning objectives do you expect an oral history project to help you to attain? How have you seen oral histories used to advantage in research, films, or exhibits? Some of your answers may change over time but it is important to remember why you find oral history exciting or intriguing, as well as the goals and expectations with which you started.

You likely came to this guide wondering, "What kind of training, experience, and resources do I need before I engage my students in an oral history project?" Professional development may take the form of a summer institute or workshop, a graduate course, or individual research and planning. (For more information on opportunities to learn about doing and teaching oral history, consult a graduate advisor in a department of history, contact the Oral History Association, or check the H-Oralhist listserv archives at http://h-net.msu.edu/~oralhist.) The following plan of individual preparation should enrich your everyday teaching, permitting you to experiment with oral history resources and materials in your classroom as you proceed.

The Introduction gave you an overview of the nature of oral history, its use in both research and public programs, and its value in teaching. Through the following activities, you and your students will learn about using oral history in the classroom. At the same time, you will build valuable instructional resources, contacts, teaching strategies, handouts, and models to initiate a successful oral history project with your students.

Using Oral History in the Classroom

Before your students undertake an oral history project, it is important that they learn about the nature of oral history. Begin with an inventory of the reading assignments and media resources that you already use, looking for examples of oral history interviews. Engage your students in discussion about the use of oral history in these examples. Encourage students to think about both what the personal narratives contribute and what other kinds of sources are needed to support, verify, or provide a context for the information that interviews provide.

Select a documentary film or videotape that features oral history interviews to show in class. Both local and national productions may be useful here, so you may want to consult your local public television sources. For example, a unit on civil rights taught in Chicago or a northern city, might include excerpts from the video *Eyes on the Prize* which is narrated by civil rights leader and historian Julian Bond along with either *Goin' to Chicago* or *Promised Land*. (Barry Lanman has produced an on-line guide for student oral history projects related to the Discovery Channel's documentary *Promised Land*.) When you show the films, ask your students to list the different sources used to document and illustrate the subject as they watch. Stop the films at several key points to discuss the sources and the information and meanings that are conveyed. Ask students to write a review of the documentary in which they discuss and assess the use of oral history interviews and other sources.

African-American Migration and the Civil Rights Movement

In order to learn and to teach about the value and characteristics of oral history, identify a topic related to the subject matter that you teach now: World War II, environmental issues, ethics and journalism, the history of aviation, etc. Survey the historical literature, documentary films, newspaper and magazine articles, Internet resources, and museum exhibits on the subject. Your research will help you to teach the subject at hand. At the same time, ask yourself questions about the use of oral history. How do interviews compare to novels, diaries and memoirs? How have oral histories contributed to our understanding of experiences and events? What are the qualities and characteristics of oral history interviews as historical documents? Bring selected examples from your research into the classroom in order to enhance your students' understanding of the past. Finally, engage your students in discussions of the same issues that you have explored in your self-directed study.

Understanding the Holocaust

Oral history has been integral to the development of Holocaust education for students and the public. Many communities have begun their own programs for recording the voices and memories of Holocaust survivors before that generation is gone. In a literature course, students may read a novel about the Holocaust like Lois Lowry's Number the Stars or Elie Wiesel's Night. Many of the most profoundly moving and revealing sources for the study of the Holocaust use oral history interviews which extend the explorations begun in these novels. These testimonies have served to make communities more aware of the history of the Holocaust and have been used as resources to confront racism, intolerance, and brutality today. The testimony of Holocaust witnesses and survivors makes tangible the crucial role of historical memory; at the same time these interviews suggest the painful dimensions of the past. It is wise to seek out representatives from local organizations both to speak to classes and to consult on the design of any Holocaust history project. For reasons of privacy and respect, which you should discuss with students, it is not appropriate to plunge into identifying and contacting local Holocaust survivors.

Oral History and the Local Scene

Local issues and community history link people to familiar landscapes, memories, and events. Identify a topic that has local implications for further study. Think about the history of your community. Read the local newspapers with an eye to local concerns and the distinctive characteristics of your community. Does heavy industry—steel, paper, or textile mill or an auto plant—dominate the local landscape? Is agriculture a mainstay of the community? Do you teach in a suburban school where new housing, highways, and shopping centers have transformed a rural landscape? Does technology drive the local economy? Have immigration and migration given rise to diverse houses of worship and ethnic festivals? Have racism and civil rights been issues that your schools have had to address? Has your community faced important planning or environmental issues in the past? Has economic change led to local unemployment and out-migration or to local growth? Is day-care an issue because more mothers are working than in the past? Is there an interesting local institution such as a sports franchise, radio station, or recording studio? Do monuments, murals, or even the names of schools, parks and streets suggest a relationship between local experience and national events?

Research the subject in local newspapers, the public library, the historical society archives, and public records. Talk with local librarians, newspaper reporters, community activists, officials, local experts, museum curators, and college faculty. Read more about the underlying issues, the historical scholarship, or the wider implications of your subject. As you look at the local implications of a problem or development, consider what personal contacts, informal interviews, and oral history resources will add to your understanding and what sources you need to complement or support the information from interviews. Develop a curriculum that integrates the local dimension, invite one of your contacts into the classroom, and then send your students out to learn more about it from people who have addressed the subject in the community.

■ *Project Suggestion*

Student access to equipment, uneasy administrators, and your own time may put significant constraints on the scope of the project. One approach is to provide students with alternatives. A family history project is often the most accessible assignment. Ask students to write a paper linking a specific individual, event or development in their family histories with wider trends and events in American history. Students may submit either a recorded oral history interview, a transcript with an introductory essay, or a research paper. The paper should run about eight pages and draw upon a variety of both primary and secondary sources, including informal interviews with family members about either their own experience or their knowledge of family history. Point out the many incentives for doing the interview, including the valuable family resource that students will produce. The interview option changes the nature of the question, "What can I write about?" engaging many students who do not see themselves as writers. Use the tape-recorded interviews in class discussions to demonstrate the nature and value of oral history to the other students. This assignment will help the class explore ideas for future themes or topics with strong local connections.

Family History Assignment

Before you launch your students on an oral history project, you may want to have some experience yourself doing oral history. Your own project will also provide resources for classroom teaching. Design a small research project; it can be about your family history, a local individual, or one of the topics that you have identified above. Follow the oral history project guidelines outlined in Chapter 3. Keep a journal of your research that includes both the data and your feelings about the experience. This will provide the materials for a model research portfolio that you can share with your students. Your students will feel more confident and may even see it as a challenge if they know that you were nervous driving to the interview or setting up your equipment. As you research the topic, scan and make overheads of the personal papers, family photographs, newspaper articles or public documents that you find most useful. Include a list of the personal contacts that you make. Show the research process in your journal: discuss the problems and dead ends that you encounter, write up and revise your interview questions, detail your contacts with the narrator before and after the

Creating a Model Portfolio

interview, describe the setting for the interview. Make at least one duplicate of each tape recording and protect the "master" recording. Write up a tape summary and a transcript of your interview. You will become personally familiar with the problems of translating from tape to type as well as with the amount of time that this will require. Select parts of the audio recordings to use in class. You may want to make an edited tape to facilitate classroom use. Review your portfolio and integrate examples from the different steps in your oral history project with your lesson plans and assignments.

This may be a good time to identify a potential archival repository for your classroom projects—contact a local library, historical society, or archives and offer to donate your recording.

After you have integrated examples of oral history into your curriculum and developed a model oral history portfolio, you may still want to engage your students in doing oral history gradually. You could start off with a small scale assignment and then move on to a larger research effort, publications or public programs, equipment purchases, and grant writing. The following chapters will walk you through projects of various scales as well as strategies for getting your students, your school administrators, and your community on board.

2

DEVELOPING AN ORAL HISTORY PROJECT

The only constraints for a classroom oral history project are the interest and enthusiasm of the teacher and the students. But given the realities of today's education, two other factors no doubt will have to be taken into account: time and cost. You might want to start with a small two-week project, using equipment available in the school. Or you might want to try a semester-long project, and apply for a grant to purchase equipment and supplies. The following chapters will show you how to do an oral history project, and will provide examples for projects which can be completed in two weeks, nine weeks, eighteen weeks, or whatever time is available. Variations on these themes are up to you.

■ *Project Suggestion*

For over twenty years, middle school teacher Michael Brooks and his students have published *Long, Long Ago,* the edited transcripts of oral history interviews that were conducted in the classroom. In order to do a school-based oral history project, invite a speaker from the local area who was involved in the events or developments that your class is studying. Provide your students with background information about the individual and ask the students to write up questions that they would like to ask. Share and discuss the questions, select a sample, and work with the students to rephrase the questions in ways that will elicit detailed and reflective answers about the narrator's own experiences. Tape-record the classroom session. Ask students to take turns working on a transcript to be edited and published in the school newspaper or literary magazine. Students should prepare an introduction to the transcript based on their readings and the background information. Make sure that you or your students share a draft of the transcript with the speaker before it is published.

An Oral History Magazine

Michael Brooks
Suva Intermediate School
6660 East Suva Street
Bell Gardens, CA 90201

Since oral history is the gathering of personal memories through recorded interviews, the experiences of the person interviewed must be first hand, not hearsay. Oral history is not folklore or legend or myth; it is the collection of information about the lifetime and the memory of the individual being asked the questions. In this guide, the person interviewed is referred to as the "narrator," and the person asking the questions is the "interviewer." Every oral history project must fit into a general context that distinguishes it from written historical research, folklore, or the random collection of engaging stories. For the classroom, it is essential to set up an oral history project with a topic that has both a clear focus and relevance to the curriculum. The importance of selecting the right project for *your* classroom cannot be stressed too much. Several factors should be considered in selecting an oral history project:

- classroom curriculum
- administrative and community support
- character and resources of the community
- budgets and funding
- focus
- scope and length

Classroom Curriculum

Where does oral history fit into the curriculum? The logical answer might seem to be social studies. But there are many other opportunities to incorporate an oral history lesson into the classroom. Oral history interviews lend themselves to many special projects for National History Day, science fairs, and other competitions that involve groups working outside of class. A drama club or student publication may undertake an oral history project, or use the results of a classroom oral history project, to develop a community play, or publish a school magazine.

■ *Project Suggestion*

National History Day

Joanne Emerick
Hoxie High School
Hoxie, KS

Oral history has come to play an extremely vital role in my students' contest entries. We are constantly searching for stories to tell. Because we've developed a reputation in this field, we continually get calls and letters from people who have topic suggestions. When an oral history topic is chosen, the students' first task is to research any pertinent subject matter. This is a yearlong effort, begun even before the students conduct their first interviews. We use books, magazines, newspapers, letters, diaries, etc. in the search for information. The bibliographies that accompany our History Day entries are often 30+ pages in length. We host open houses to share our oral history presentations with the public and are also invited to make presentations at numerous locations statewide. We seek not only to collect oral histories, but also to share and preserve them.

For my students and me, the use of oral history makes the past come alive. An oral history was conducted with New Hampshire resident Angela Matthews, who in 1968 lost her fiancé in Vietnam. Angela and seven others from across the nation who suffered similar losses participated in a series of phone interviews with three students and myself. We discussed the significance of the Vietnam Wall and its healing powers. We listened as they remembered their loved ones, cried over their loss, and said that by sharing their memories with us, they could insure future healing. Our interviews resulted in a national award-winning program called "If you look at it with your heart, you know the story."

Practices in Oral History

A natural place for an oral history project, of course, is the history or social studies classroom. Here the focus can be on content. The subject might be an event, a process, an era, or an individual. In a psychology class, the emphasis might be memory itself, or perhaps the ways in which individuals react to or handle an event or crisis. In a sociology class, the focus might be on a group reaction, for example how a union or a company faces a strike action. A study of the dimensions of contemporary women's work, in an economics class, could begin with the documentary, "A Midwife's Tale" (aired on the PBS series *American Experience*) and student discussion of the varied contexts for and the nature of women's work as represented in the film. History, political science, sociology, psychology and the sciences may come into play if the project examines how a community is forced to change because of some outside force such as urban renewal or a natural disaster.

In health education classes, an oral history project may provide a community service. Young people can visit the elderly in housing units or nursing homes and interview people about their lives or careers, exploring the secrets of long and productive lives. Or they can learn about aging and disease. One of the rather magical aspects of young people interviewing the elderly is the emotional bond that often develops between them. Students asked about their interviews often described the "two sides," or the "two personalities" of the narrator. The students are referring to the elderly person they see in front of them, and the other person they "see" as the narrator reveals stories from the past.

In science classes a good use of oral history is to have students interview physicists, chemists, biologists, medical workers or others about their research and careers. Another project might be to interview a variety of residents about a local environmental issue such as contamination of the water supply or destruction of wildlife habitat. Community members, elected officials, consulting engineers, leaders of interest groups, and experts from a nearby university could all help students understand that their science studies can be related to a real community issue.

Most of the projects I directed took place in English classrooms. The reasons for this are twofold: the English curriculum is flexible, and it is process-oriented. The topics for an oral history can be just about anything if the rationale is to teach communication skills rather than a specific subject. To prepare for any oral history project, students must research, read, listen, and reflect. They learn interviewing skills and writing skills, and, in the process, read a lot of good literature. Novels, plays, short stories, essays and poetry easily support and enhance historical research for just about any oral history topic. The emphasis is on the communication process and the final product, using the historical subject as the means to that end.

None of these topics needs to be confined to a particular curriculum; oral history is an excellent tool in interdisciplinary, team-taught courses. Oral history projects also lend themselves to cooperative learning. Teamwork often results in fewer and thus more manageable and more successful oral histories than individual assignments. Students may work together at each step in the process: preparing, conducting, transcribing, and presenting the results of the interview. Students can then share among the groups the responsibilities for summarizing and transcribing each other's interviews. As a result, more students will be familiar with the content of each interview when it comes time to discuss the results of the project in class.

■ Project Suggestion

Analyzing and Organizing Interview Content

Rich Nixon
South Johnson High School
Four Oaks, NC

The students first determined what topics they wanted to investigate under the broad umbrella of "teenage life," and then brainstormed various questions for each topic. Each student was required to audiotape interviews of two people who had been teenagers during the 1950s and had lived in the school district at that time, and then transcribe the interviews. After this was completed, we scheduled time into our school's computer composition lab and each student entered his or her transcript into the computer. We then divided the class into editorial groups, with each group focusing on one aspect of growing up, and circulated the transcripts of the interviews among the groups. The groups pulled from the transcripts portions relevant to their areas of interest. These areas later became the chapters of our book, Cruisin'.

Careful attention to developmental sequencing and opportunities to re-hearse, to expand upon, and to reflect on new knowledge is crucial for individual student growth. Oral history adds new dimensions to almost any academic subject: interviews with scientists about their research will rein-force student understanding of the scientific method. Student understanding of immigration over time can be expanded and strengthened by making connections to the migrations that have shaped the local community. For example, one student's grandmother describes her feelings after the move from a Kentucky coal mining camp to Franklin, Ohio: "It began to get close to spring and I began to get homesick. It took me a long time to get satisfied in Ohio." She returned to Kentucky with her children until her husband found them a house on a farm and then a neighbor brought them to Ohio:

"I had bought me a pig. I loved livestock, but my little pig was dead when we unloaded . . . My pig, that just ruined my day." The interview invites questions about the painful costs of dislocation that are often submerged in larger narratives of opportunity.

Oral history is a powerful tool in developing written and oral communication skills. Students have to think carefully about how questions are worded. They learn that the phrasing of a question may lead, intimidate, irritate, or even offend the narrator. During the interview, the student listens attentively, absorbing the information, and following through with appropriate questions or comments. English teachers often complain that students say they have nothing to write about. Oral histories provide both content and purpose for writing assignments. Students can write a description of the interview setting; write an introduction to the narrator's life and times; or write a summary of the content of the interview. If there is a transcript of all or part of the interview, students may write a synthesis or analysis of what they learned in the form of a paper, exhibit, or presentation.

Oral history projects can be used to enhance interdisciplinary team teaching and to integrate writing, communications, and technology across the curriculum. It has been used successfully with remedial students, students in general classes, and with gifted students. There have been several successful projects integrated into English as a Second Language classes.

■ *Project Suggestion*

Research on language learning and teaching emphasizes the importance of talk as a way to develop and enhance students' other language skills. This is especially important for remedial/non-academic students who may be weak in reading and writing abilities, yet may possess strong oral language skills. Unfortunately, the students who could most benefit from enriched language experiences that capitalize on their language strengths are usually placed in traditional remedial or general classes where there is a strong emphasis on grammar and skills, little talk, and where the student is a passive participant. In this project, the students are paired with older members of the community and spend several hour-long sessions working with them. To prepare for these meetings, the students read and discuss materials related to older people in society. The students then develop questions that they feel are significant to ask their older partners. The questions are evaluated and categorized by the students for use during the interviews. The interviews are taped and loosely transcribed by the students and then the students are asked to develop several different types of writing as a result of this experience. The writings are published in a booklet and a copy of this booklet is given to all the participants at a special meeting.

Inter-Generational Interviewing

Nancy Lubarsky
Abraham Clark High School
Roselle, NJ

No matter what subject you teach there are numerous possible oral history projects, limited only by the enthusiasm of the teacher and the students. Although the teacher will want to limit the choices, the students should participate in the decision process. Involving the students from the start will ensure their excitement and interest through the entire project. Without their support, they may be reluctant scholars quick to complain about the "extra" work. If they understand the value of the project, and the importance of their role in it, they will give more than is required to the effort.

■ *Project Suggestion*

Meeting Content and Performance Standards

Martha Evans
David Hartle-Schutte
Kahealani Nae'ole-Wong
Keaukaha Elementary School, HI

This 1997 project took advantage of oral history to tap the "wealth of knowledge and stories . . . in the hearts and minds of the elders," and to foster connections between students, parents, grandparents and other community members. At the same time, the teachers aimed to improve student oral and written language skills through the process of collecting these stories. As a result of the project, students will:

- Demonstrate improved communication skills: listening, speaking, reading, writing
- Gain competence in basic interviewing skills
- Develop a written product based on an oral interview
- Compare common events from the past with current everyday events
- Gain an appreciation for differences between life today and life in the past
- Develop a deeper understanding of the changes that have occurred in the community or family life
- Develop closer connections to family and community members
- Create multimedia products incorporating written, visual and auditory elements

View the project description of the semester long project for fourth to sixth grade students at http://www.k12.hi.us/`keaukaha/oral_hist.proj/intro.html.

Administrative and Community Support

Carefully consider the school administration's support for your project. Since students will be going into the community to interview the narrators, the school administration must be aware of the project, its rationale, which students are involved, and what will be done with the final project. Anticipate their questions about risks, obstacles, and ethical problems that may arise. If money is needed to cover costs, it is important to keep the administrators informed and involved, preferably well in advance of the financial request. Ten steps to build and ensure administrative and community support:

1 Design the scope and goals of the project to meet specific curriculum goals that your school system must address.

2 Informally discuss the idea with your department chair and be sure he/she is supportive.

3 Create a syllabus, handouts, and/or lesson plans for the unit.

4 Prepare a budget and discuss internal and outside funding opportunities with your chair and other administrators.

5 Discuss the project with your principal, and have your department chair attend. Present the syllabus and budget to site-based management or curriculum committees within the school as well.

6 Notify the school superintendent and/or the school board by letter, and, if necessary, set up a meeting to discuss the project.

7 Consult area newspaper, radio, and television reporters both for their expertise in the subject and to ensure public recognition for the project.

8 Use the project to build or straighten connections between your school, local government, college faculty, the chamber of commerce, area businesses, and community organizations.

9 Keep the school administration informed throughout the project, forward news stories and information on community contacts as the projects unfolds, and prepare a final report.

10 Invite administrators and representatives of local organizations to public programs showcasing the project and give public recognition to their support.

The help and understanding of the students' families is critical for maintaining administrative and community support. Talk the project over with the students and be sure they have a part in selecting the topic or narrowing the focus. Send the parents a letter describing the project, the learning objectives, the tasks involved, and the basis for assessing student work. A similar letter can introduce the student and the project to potential narrators (see Handout 4). For longer and more extensive oral history projects, invite the students and their parents to attend an evening meeting to discuss the project and answer questions. Parents often volunteer their services and become valuable supporters, helping locate narrators and resource materials, and helping with transportation.

It goes without saying, if the first oral history project is a success, more community support will follow. Middle school teacher Michael Brooks recommends "publicity, publicity, and more publicity" to enhance both student enthusiasm for the project and community support. A multimedia presentation in Middletown, Ohio, resulted in a show that summed up the project for the students and provided a valuable vehicle for obtaining recognition from the community. Submitting a successful project for a professional award or presenting a paper on the project at a professional meeting can also garner institutional support.

School Histories—Two Projects

Pamela Dean
T. Harry Williams Oral History Center
University of Louisiana

An oral history of the school is a good starting point for an oral history program. School histories touch upon significant local and national historical developments such as changing theories of education, family and economic change, migration and population shifts, gender roles, school desegregation, and civil rights. At the same time, a school history provides a rationale for interviewing and renewing ties to alumnae and former staff and teachers. In Baton Rouge, a student oral history of an urban high school through the T. Harry Williams Oral History Center at University of Louisiana brought local traditional blues musicians back into the school. A school history project may enhance public recognition of, support for, and involvement in the schools while offering current students a glimpse of the accomplishments as well as the problems faced and decisions made by previous generations of students. The Oral History Center went on to sponsor high school student oral history projects documenting the history of area churches and businesses.

Lisa Rowe Fraustino
Wyoming Seminary Lower School

On the first day of school, fifth grades at Wyoming Seminary Lower School walked into an English classroom that already had a question written on the board, "What was fifth grade like fifty years ago?" Students answered the question in a trimester-long oral history project. After studying interviewing techniques and practicing their own interviewing skills with each other and with parents, fifth graders each interviewed someone of their own choice—a relative, neighbor, or teacher—who was in fifth grade at least fifty years ago. They shaped their interview notes into essays that they revised, edited, proofread, and self-published in a book called *Fifth Grade Fifty Years Ago*.

The Character and Resources of the Community

Communities provide the resources that sustain and support the schools, socially as well as financially. A school is a microcosm of the community in which it exists. An oral history project can connect the school and the community in ways that few other classroom projects do. Every community has a cultural heritage, which is a composite of history, buildings, environment, religion, events, and lifestyles; a world of differences and similarities. What is the character of your community? Discuss the questions under Oral History and the Local Scene in Chapter One with your students.

■ *Project Suggestion*

Explore the shape and character of your community. Use documentary films with oral history interviews to spark discussions of possible local research topics. Have your students read the local newspapers and talk about the community with their parents or neighbors. Ask students to brainstorm a list of potential oral history topics. Assign students a brief paper describing the school community, including some of the ideas they have read or talked about.

The cultural heritage of your community or region will be the starting point. Ask your students to think strategically about the research. Help your students identify specific resources for studying selected topics. As you and your students narrow the choices, work with school and public librarians to search out information and documents. Use the networks that you have, including parents, school administrators, fellow teachers, and contacts with community organizations, local reporters, and librarians to identify both resources and potential narrators for your project. Community foundations are a source of both expertise on the character of the community and potential funding.

Money always helps a project run smoothly. Outside funding can be used for **Funding** many things: film rentals, the purchase of additional resources (books, equipment, etc.), guest speakers, a stipend for a scholar/adviser, rental of equipment, transcribing the interviews, designing and printing a publication, rental of a place to hold a public forum, and all those "little extras" like postage, copies, duplicate cassettes, etc. The list could go on!

Although an oral history project can run on a "shoestring," you might want to cast around for outside funding sources. It requires energy, initiative, and aggressiveness on your part, but the rewards are worth it. How much money depends on the project you have planned. Some potential sources of funds and support include the state humanities council, local colleges and universities, local businesses and foundations, as well as state education funds.

Each state has a humanities council (sometimes called a humanities committee or a humanities board) which receives an annual grant of money from the National Endowment for the Humanities. Each state council establishes its own guidelines for funding what they call "regrants." The state committee meets several times during the year to review applications and fund projects. Obviously, the primary consideration for a grant from the humanities council is an application with a strong humanities content. If you are seeking funds to support an oral history project you have met at least a part of that requirement because "history" is one of the humanities. Check with your state council for their application guidelines. As mentioned before, the Rhode Island Committee for the Humanities provided part of the funding for the five oral history projects described in the Introduction. The grants ranged from slightly under $10,000 to more than $14,000. The funds paid for scholars, speakers, text resources, rental of equipment, the printed publication, public forums, and related expenses. The grants were matched by "in kind" contributions, mainly the time the teacher and I spent on the project, but also by the scholars who donated half their time.

Colleges and universities have a number of human and material resources available to the public, especially those schools that are publicly supported. University professors often provide "community service" as project advisers. They are willing to come to the classroom as guest speakers, or to share their expertise in planning a project, or to suggest primary and secondary resources for the research. College students may also have "service learning" or community service requirements, which can be met as project volunteers.

My projects have always used "humanist scholars" to help with the historical content of the research and to meet the grant guidelines of the state humanities council. The scholars have worked right along with the students, helping to prepare the questionnaire identifying the historical significance of the interviews, helping the students focus their narratives, writing scholarly essays for the publication, and discussing the project with the students at several points during the process.

Another university resource is technical expertise. I was fortunate to find a group at a private university whose mission is to create educational resources on the Internet. The group welcomed the opportunity to work with a classroom of students who were actively engaged in a local history project. They provided digital audio equipment, advised the students on technical aspects, and folded the research and interviews into a site on the Internet. Photographs taken by a student photographer and photographs loaned by the narrators were incorporated into the web site. Colleges may also provide audiovisual assistance, and can sometimes loan equipment to the schools in their communities. College publication departments may be able to offer advice or provide services. It's worth asking! But be sure you know specifically and in detail what it is you want from them. You'll get better results if you have a short and specific request. At the very least, the colleges and universities may provide the archival repository for the finished oral history project. Chances are the library has a "Special Collections Department" which is probably the right place for this primary source material.

Private foundations or endowments are more numerous than you might think. Locating the addresses and phone numbers for them is often the hard part. Consult the school development officer, the humanities council, the state historical society, the local historical society, the public library, the Internet, and even the Yellow Pages for a listing of foundations. Make a phone call to ascertain if it might be a possible funding source, and if it is, write a letter describing the project and exactly what you would like them to provide (cash, equipment, etc.) Be sure it meets the foundation's guidelines.

Write the letter on school letterhead. As with almost any proposal, contact the organization well in advance of the deadline and seek its help and suggestions. If they turn you down, ask for feedback and revise your proposal.

Education funds may be available for your project. For example, federal "Title" funds are designated for specific target groups such as drug and alcohol prevention programs. Federal funds may be targeted for students who have difficulty reading or to support programs for the elderly. Perhaps an oral history project in a health, science or social studies class would meet the requirements? With a little ingenuity and creativity, you might be able to make a match.

State departments of education often have programs they are developing or reworking. Sometimes they channel federal monies to the local communities or counties, but they may also have funds from the state legislature earmarked for special programs or for innovative initiatives. What's more innovative than a classroom oral history project? There seems to be more and more money available on the state level for technology from educational initiatives. There may be an opportunity for additional funds if your oral history project has an Internet component.

Of course, there is always the tried and true way of working the oral history project right into the classroom curriculum and developing a department budget for it. Given the current status of school funding, this may be a far reach, but perhaps it's the best way to ensure a future for oral history projects in the classroom.

An oral history project should have a specific focus. Picking the topic and **Focus for the Project**
achieving consensus among your students is a challenging process. Once you get started, it is likely you will have too many ideas rather than too few. You may determine the focus in advance (this is particularly likely if you plan to pursue outside funding in advance for the project) or in concert with your students. Oral history projects usually fall into the following categories, which may overlap:
- an event (for example, a strike, a political campaign, or a natural disaster)
- an issue (for example, racism, or a decision to build a power plant)
- a topic (for example, a local musical tradition, a hobby, a business, local houses of worship, a community organization, a neighborhood or park)

- an individual (for example, the life stories of individuals over a certain age, or the stories of multiple generations in a family)
- a historical era (for example, the Great Depression, the Vietnam War years, the 1950's, or even a year like 1968)

You will want to either agree upon one common research topic for a class oral history project or divide the students into teams pursuing several topics. The first option will produce a more cohesive final project; the latter will allow students to pursue projects of particular interest. The narrower the focus, the easier it is to adapt the project to the curriculum, and the easier it is for the students to complete the project successfully.

It is important to start your project with something or some things that you want to find out about. Generally, a topic is inexhaustible, you can continue to collect information, particularly interviews, about immigration or race relations in your community for years. If you pose a problem or a question, your students can more readily judge both what information is pertinent and how much information is enough. You could ask, what problems did immigrant children face in the public schools? Or, what strategies did local civil rights activists use to advance their cause? You must also define the scope of the project in a way that makes oral history central to your study. You may learn a great deal about the civil rights movement from newspapers or the minutes of school board meetings. Interviews, however, can tell you about how people now look back and assess the strategies, goals, and accomplishments of the movement.

In class discussions, students use critical thinking skills to identify a "research-able topic" and to focus the topic into a manageable research project. The topic must be something that can be researched within your community, and you should keep in mind the age and mobility of both your students and the narrators. Another consideration is the sophistication of the students, their ability to ask questions, and the ease with which they can understand the topic.

Although similar in format, each of the five classroom projects that I directed was entirely different in focus. The first was a topic (town meeting government); the second, an event (a natural disaster); the third, a historical era (limited to female narrators); the fourth, an entire decade; the fifth, a year of extremes. The easiest one for the students was the "Hurricane" project because it focused on a single event on one day in one year. Perhaps the most difficult one, in terms of research and focus, was the "1950's" project because it dealt with so many issues, events, people and places over a decade that actually stretched from 1946 to 1963! The most rewarding oral history was "Grandma," because of its significant historical value as well as its unique focus on the role of women during the war, an area neglected by many history textbooks. The most interesting project for me was the "1968" project. I had experienced it, but never really understood it from a historical perspective. The collection of eyewitness accounts gave me a first-hand knowledge of the complexity of American politics and life in the late 1960's.

■ *Project Suggestion*

Brainstorm possible topics with the students, making a list of suggestions on the chalkboard. Discuss the ideas that emerge and cross out the least popular ones, ranking the others by group consensus priority. Ask the students to explore the topics in small groups, writing down related ideas and names or descriptions of potential narrators. Make a tentative choice of the top two or three project ideas, and ask the students to come in the next day with reasons why one of the topics should be chosen. Select the one best supported by the students.

Scope and Length of the Project

The length of class time you can devote to an oral history unit will determine the scope of the project that your students can complete. Some of the factors that influence the length of the project include:

- the number of narrators each student can interview
- the depth or length of interviews and the number of questions to be asked
- the effort that can be devoted to selecting narrators
- the depth of research which can be done on the topic
- the extent to which the project can be integrated into the subject curriculum
- whether or not there is outside funding available for consultants, speakers, films, etc.
- the nature of the interview questions
- whether transcripts or only tape indexes can be produced to supplement the recorded interview
- the nature of the final product that students complete
- the opportunities for public programs and publicity

The following suggestions will help you implement a classroom oral history ranging from a two-week project to a semester-long project.

A two-week unit must have a simple focus and design. There should be one brief set of common questions, no more than one person for each student to interview, and one simple assignment to present the results. There will be little time to research a difficult topic or plan how to approach it, or to choose narrators. You can introduce students to the basic techniques of oral history. The students can, in turn, have a valuable experience of meeting and learning from the narrator. One way to arrange such a brief project would be to have the students pick a relative or neighbor as a narrator. The criteria for selection can be broad, such as: "Interview any relative or neighbor who is over 70 years old about his/her experiences as a high school student." Or the criteria could be specific: "Identify a person who served in the Vietnam War and find out how the experience has affected his/her life, for better or worse." Because tape recordings are opaque and thus difficult for subsequent researchers to access, the assignment must include at least an index of the interview content.

A four-week unit will work like the two-week unit, but will allow some time to prepare and to research the topic, and possibly to do some outside reading related to the subject. Teachers can use this short unit to reinforce a classroom lesson from a personal experience. For example, students in a science class who are studying earthquakes could read a chapter from John McPhee's book, *Assembling California,* discuss it, and write a set of questions to find out what it's really like to experience an earthquake. A mark on the Richter scale is nothing compared to eyewitness accounts and personal anecdotes. The results could be presented in written first person accounts of the disaster, as a reenactment, or as a short videotaped news report.

A nine-week unit permits greater flexibility. One quarter of the school year provides time for more preparation and research; perhaps more than one set of questions; a choice of narrators; a practice interview, and two assigned (or chosen) interviews. The final product to present the results of the oral history project might have several parts, which might include a public forum or a publication produced through desktop publishing.

For example, your students could learn about the ethnicity of their community, by exploring family histories. Starting with their own families, students could create family trees depicting the names and nationalities of their ancestors. Next, they could research their ancestors' countries of origin, collecting descriptions, making maps, finding recipes, photographs, postcards saved in family scrapbooks, or found in libraries or the historical society. They could read related articles or essays, or possibly short stories or poetry.

Although each student might want to develop his or her own set of questions based on the country of origin, the class could work together on the questions common to all the interviews. The students may choose to interview someone who was born in another country (possibly of the student's own ethnicity), but who immigrated to the United States. For the final report, each student could write an article for a classroom or school newsletter or newspaper, and illustrate it with photographs, drawings and other reproductions. The project might end with a reception for the narrators featuring foods from the different ethnic groups represented.

■ *Project Suggestion*

Ask your students to find out where their parents, grandparents, and great-grandparents were born and raised. Make a list of regions of the country and the world and conduct a census in class, using student assistants to tally the numbers for each generation and region. (In southern Ohio, the impact of a massive, mid-twentieth century migration from Appalachia becomes immediately evident.) Ask students to first identify patterns, trends, and exceptions for discussion, and then to assess the validity of your classroom population as a sample of the community or region. A mathematics or computer programming class might turn the results into an interesting spreadsheet while a history class can learn more about the impact of the past on the present.

A semester-long oral history project can be most extensively integrated with the standard curriculum. In addition, teachers may want to modify their assignments and texts to fit the focus of the project. For example, in an English class that did an oral history project about World War II, students read *Rumors of Peace* by Ella Lefland and the play *All My Sons* by Arthur Miller while guest speakers and selected films augmented the research. There was time to carefully select the narrators to represent a variety of roles appropriate to the topic, reflecting a composite of community experiences and responses. In a semester project, students will want to compare and discuss the issues and the interviews as they proceed, gathering more information and learning from each other. The final results might be as elaborate as a web site, a publication with stories and photographs, a video, or a multimedia presentation; or as simple as a set of transcripts and stories.

When the topic of the oral history has been chosen and its length and breadth has been determined, ask the students to write a clear and brief statement of purpose. Work with the students to make sure they understand exactly what the project's focus is. Using the sample as a guide, assign a letter of introduction for homework that will incorporate the statement of purpose. Have the students discuss the idea with their parents, relatives, and neighbors. Ask them to collect newspaper articles of related stories, and draw up a list of the kinds of narrators needed to explore the subject: gender, occupation, religion, race, ethnicity. Ask the students to compare their lists with others in the class. Begin to assemble the database of potential narrators.

3

THE ORAL HISTORY PROJECT

This chapter provides a step-by-step procedure for implementing a classroom oral history project from background research to the final product.

Oral history is more than asking questions. It's asking the right questions. The only way to do that is to do research. Here are some suggestions.

**Developing a
Knowledge Base**

Start in your school library media center. Using both electronic and print media, students can locate articles, books and other resources valuable to the project. The Internet adds a valuable dimension to the students' media search. In many school media centers students also have access to the public and to the university electronic catalogs.

Check with area museums for relevant exhibits. Local and state historical societies offer a wealth of archival and primary source material. Photographs, maps, diaries, letters, and minutes of meetings can reveal history as it was happening. Librarians and archivists are more than willing to share the resources with high school students. Students learn of otherwise "invisible" resources. It is a lesson in preservation as students witness the care given to these original documents. For the "Hurricane" project, the state historical society provided invaluable aerial photographs and snapshots taken the day after the storm, which dramatically documented the complete destruction of the homes on the barrier beaches and in downtown Providence. The larger newspapers also have archives, a resource seldom tapped by either high school teachers or students. Sometimes valuable information can appear in the most unlikely and least expected places. At the local newspaper office of *The Westerly Sun,* the publisher pulled open a bottom drawer of his desk to show us a box crammed with snapshots sent in by readers in the weeks following the hurricane of 1938. There they had been for forty years!

Guest speakers knowledgeable about historical events or local history offer another interesting aspect of research. Use the networks and contacts that you have developed in preparing for and planning the oral history project. Most of your guests will be happy to come and share their backgrounds with your students, and will not ask a fee. If it the topic is Vietnam, invite a veteran, a woman nurse, a conscientious objector, and a war protestor to talk to the students. If there is a college nearby, call the relevant department chair, describe your project, and ask for a referral to someone with expertise in that area; then invite the faculty member to talk about the topic's historical background with your class. With permission, record the guest speaker and the question and answer period.

There will also be relevant cultural aspects to your students' research—films, music, and art of the period will add to the students' understanding and enthusiasm. When we studied the American family in the 1950's, we invited the top disc jockey from that era to come and speak to the students. He told of meeting Elvis, Bill Haley, and other rock and roll musicians, and he played selections from the "Top 40" songs of the era, which thrilled the students. Films, videos, slides, and documentaries were other important resources; for example, advertisements and films of the fifties demonstrated how fashions reflected the culture. For the "Grandma" project, we showed the documentary Rosie the Riveter and a feature film from the forties, Mrs. Miniver. For the 1950's project, we showed West Side Story as well as Duck and Cover, a short documentary about what to do if there was an atomic bomb warning.

■ *Project Suggestion*

**"Hangin' in our 'hoods":
Oral History and Seventh Grade Geography**

*Donnalynn Sharer
E. S. Miller Remedial/
Discipline Public School
Philadelphia, PA*

Students in this school came from many different Philadelphia neighborhoods. This unit began with an introduction to using maps (compass, measurement, map symbols, map key, etc.) For this project, we used Philadelphia street maps, mass transit maps, and maps of Delaware Valley and Pennsylvania. Students created grid maps of the area around the school and the neighborhoods. They researched the origin of at least four street names in each neighborhood. We used the African American Historical Marker Guide to find out about at least ten people/places which are featured with markers, and made flyers to advertise for an event that could occur at the marker location. We used census data to find out population, ethnic diversity, and household income for each neighborhood. Then the students put together profiles of the neighborhoods, including government offices, religious institutions, commercial areas, schools, recreation centers, parks, and hangouts. The project included an oral history component as well. Students listened to a sample interview and then wrote interview questions in groups. The questions focused on physical and social features of the neighborhood, physical and social changes over time, ways to improve the neighborhood, efforts to improve the neighborhood, and high points of the neighborhood.

During the research period, students and teacher should begin to compile a list of potential narrators, starting with names that appear in the documents or that crop up through contacts. Notify the local newspapers about the project and suggest an article. Prepare a press release. Consider placing an advertisement in the newspaper or printing flyers, which can be distributed in the community through the public libraries and museums. Students are usually very good at getting the word out. Sometimes just publicizing it in the school is helpful. The more the students learn about the topic, the more they will talk about it—with friends, family, relatives, neighbors, and others in the community. This often results in a deluge of names. Keep a record of the names, phone numbers, addresses of potential narrators, and a thumb-nail description (where she was, what he was doing, how she was identified as a narrator, etc.) for each person either on index cards or in a database. I actually use both index cards and a database.

As the project becomes more clearly defined, you will need to make several important decisions about whom to interview. Refer back to the focus and scope of the project to help with the selection of narrators. In the case of our "Grandma" project, we had determined from the start that we would focus only on women. It then became clear we would need to interview women who represented the variety of jobs and roles that women filled during the war years, both in the war and on the home front. We identified nurses, Red Cross workers, civil defense workers, and even one woman who had served with the United Service Organization (USO). Along the way we discovered a woman who played baseball "in a league of their own" and another who flew airplanes, one who was a pacifist and another who through her university work with plants discovered a way to keep sand from blowing on the airport runways. We wanted to interview Jews, Protestants, Catholics, and minorities. Although no selection process could ever be a perfect sample, each project should always aim for a fair representation.

For the 1950's oral history, we expanded the narrator pool to include age diversity as well as social, gender, religious and racial diversity. We chose some narrators who were teenagers in the 1950's, others who were parents, and a few adults involved in important issues of the times, such as civil rights and civil liberties.

For the 1968 project, we identified key issues and sought narrators who could speak from experience about those issues. Some of the narrators included: a former governor who had led the Robert Kennedy delegation to the Chicago convention, Vietnam veterans who both supported and opposed the war, a draft resister who went to Canada and then returned to seek sanctuary in a church, a former POW and his wife, and a conscientious objector. Narrators were selected to talk about the major themes—civil rights, politics, women's issues, popular culture and the Vietnam War.

Ora Cooks, Professor of Education at Clark Atlanta University uses the "Witness to History" survey form (Handout 2) to explore topics with her students. The students can examine the history that they themselves have witnessed and then go out and ask others to respond to the survey. The results suggest potential research topics and narrators while the students learn to see themselves and others as part of history.

It is important to send each potential narrator a letter explaining the purpose of the project (see Handout 4). Be sure to explain that all potential narrators may not be interviewed. A Narrator Information Form (Handout 3) helps in selecting the narrators. You might even include one or two of the questions so the person can reflect on them, and perhaps help them to think about some artifacts he may have kept. I have always mailed the forms with the letter that explains the project (Handout 4). Some oral historians recommend meeting the narrators before setting up the interview. I have found that logistically this is difficult to do in student projects, and it is also time consuming. The advantage of the pre-interview is that the student meets the narrator face to face and gets to know him or her a little before the interview. The student will have a better idea of how to focus the questions for that narrator. Again, use the Narrator Information Form to help select the narrators for the project.

Matching the student with the narrator is something you can do in different ways. I have asked the students to read the Information Forms of the narrators, and to select the one or two persons they are most interested in interviewing. Sometimes students are satisfied to have the teacher make the selection. If the students have met the narrator in a pre-interview than they may want to make their choice based on that. In the 1968 project the students said during the final evaluation they would have liked to have known whom they would be interviewing (or the role of the person—soldier, protestor, woman's rights, African-American, etc.) before they started the research. They felt they could have concentrated their research more on that particular aspect of the person's background, and asked better follow-up questions during the interview.

The student will contact the person by telephone and set up the time and place for the interview, writing it down on the Information Sheet. If the interview is a few weeks away, the student should call to remind the narrator a few days before.

A master schedule of interviews should be posted in the classroom. If equipment is being shared, the schedule must reflect the availability of the equipment. I have always assembled a "kit" of information to go with each student to the interview. It includes the questions, the Legal Release Form, instructions on using the equipment, tips reminding the student how to ask the questions, and some notepaper and a pencil.

■ *Project Suggestion*

Give the students a list of potential narrators, which has been compiled during the research and formulating question phase of the project. Have the students establish criteria for selection of narrators, based on their earlier discussions, and write the criteria on the chalkboard. Ask the class to rank the persons on the list using a 1–5 numerical rating, 5 being the best.

Research Ethics

An important issue in any oral history project is protecting the rights of both the narrator and the interviewer. Universities and colleges often require a project review by a Committee for Research with Human Subjects. These institutional review boards stem from past incidents of abuse of research subjects in medical and psychological studies; however, the review process has been extended to other fields of research involving people. While such reviews are rare for school-based projects, you and your students should consider the welfare and interests of project narrators. Discuss how interviews and public programs may impact on the people interviewed and their families. Narrators should be assured of their right to refuse or to withdraw from the project at any time. Make sure that the narrator receives a letter describing the project and plans for public programs before students conduct interviews.

The words spoken in an oral history project become an important record of history, part of the historical documentation; these words are also the property of the narrator. Regardless of whether the information will be published or presented to the public for the project, it is essential that the information be released in a formal and legal agreement, which will protect all participants. The narrator has the right to restrict use of the interview, or to exclude parts of it, or to remain anonymous. The issues of rights and consent provide a valuable opportunity to introduce students to ethical issues in research.

For many reasons, including the copyright law, there must be a Legal Release Form (Handout 7), signed by the narrator and the interviewer. *Oral History and the Law* by John Neuenschwander (No. 1 in the Oral History Association Pamphlet Series) clearly explains the legal and ethical issues involved with an oral history project. The Oral History Association guidelines are now available on the OHA website (noted in the bibliography). The student should explain the legal release form and answer any questions the narrator might ask. Both narrator and interviewer must sign the agreement in each other's presence. Occasionally the narrator might wish to check with an attorney or review the interview transcript before signing the form. The original copy should be kept with the master audiocassette, index, and transcript, if there is one. Copies of the Legal Release should accompany any subsequent copies and secondary materials. Oral histories on the World Wide Web present additional issues of copyright and preservation.

It is also important to inform the narrator of any public programs. In class discuss how narrators might feel about their roles and/or participation. While a narrator's feelings will rarely preclude a full and just representation of the information collected, students can learn important lessons from this process. Whether or not you ask the narrator to review the transcript is up the teacher. In the projects I have conducted we have not given the narrators the transcripts for several reasons: lack of sufficient time, the cost of copying the transcript and mailing it, and finally, the concern of getting the transcript back from the narrator and making his or her corrections. Once, during the "Hurricane of '38" project, a former Governor requested the transcript. When he returned it to us, two-thirds of it had been crossed out with a purple marker.

Remember two things: a good interviewer is curious, and a good interviewer is an involved listener. Not all people make good interviewers. However, most young adults make wonderful interviewers. Their natural curiosity combined with good listening skills (which can be taught) are a win-win combination.

Studs Terkel espouses a jazz theory of interviewing. Like good jazz, there is a theme to follow, a beginning, middle, and an end. But the interviewer will need to improvise and allow the music to go off in a variety of directions, provided it remains consistent to the theme, and returns to it again and again. Like jazz, improvisation is difficult and it is a skill not all people have. It requires knowledge of the material and confidence in oneself. Students, although lacking in the maturity of age, have the confidence of youth and the spontaneity to go for it, without the inhibitions many adults have. They will miss some follow-up questions in an interview, but most interviewers miss points. The important thing is that the students will get a lot of information, and they will often pick up information an adult might have overlooked. Another factor that emerges in student oral history interviews is that the narrator often takes the role of mentor, and feels an obligation to share knowledge with the younger generation. This age-old relationship pays off in dividends in an oral history project.

There are two kinds of questions: open and closed. Except to pinpoint a specific date or time, clarify a point, or identify a person or event, all the questions should be open-ended. Questions that are too specific (such as dates) may make the narrator uncomfortable. An open-ended question elicits a narrative response, one in which the narrator will be encourage to recall an episode, an anecdote, or a description of a person or a place. The importance of the questions cannot be overstated. What you get in response to the questions will provide the critical mass for the oral history project. (Handout 8)

Have the class discuss how to compile these questions and structure the topics. The final form of the question format should be left up to the teacher. There may be separate questions for the men and for the women, or there may be both common questions and the flexibility to pursue more individualized topics. In our fifties project, we had separate questions for teens and for parents. For our "Grandma" project, we had separate questions for women who went into the military during the war, for those who worked outside the home, and for those who were either homemakers or in school or college at the time. In the 1968 project we asked a number of questions about the narrator's life growing up which seemed to sidetrack some of the narrators, bogging them down in irrelevant information. Many of these questions were eliminated in the revised questionnaire for the second interviews, resulting in an interview more focused on the issues and events of 1968. Some questions may need to be modified, some omitted, and others added to clarify the focus and ensure a content that will be meaningful and relevant. The students' feedback on their interviews is an important ingredient in this process.

■ *Project Suggestion*

Using the research, and perhaps the outside expertise of a knowledgeable person (another teacher or a scholar from the community), ask the students to list issues that should be covered. Discuss what kinds of questions can best elicit detailed responses. Divide the class into groups and give each group two or three issues on which to prepare questions. Have each group write 5 to 10 questions on each issue and discuss the questions that best address the issue. For homework ask them to write 20 to 30 additional questions, organized around the topics. Ask them to include at least one of each type of question. You may want to suggest an 80/20 split between open and closed questions. Remind the students that the emphasis is always on what the narrator knows first hand, or has witnessed himself, as well as his/her own interpretation of those events. Oral history is not retelling information learned second hand, but is always first hand point of view and observation.

The Practice Interview   While the students are scheduling their first interviews, the teacher should plan a practice interview for the classroom. It can easily be fit into one class period. Choose someone you know will be comfortable being interviewed in front of the class, and someone who meets the criteria for the narrator in this project. You might consider a teacher in the school or a retired teacher for the practice interview. The day before, ask for three student volunteers, and have them prepare a section of questions, just as though it was for a real interview. In addition to the audio recording, it is recommended that the practice interview be videotaped, using an external microphone and a camcorder on a tripod. Introduce the narrator to the class, and have the first student interviewer set up the tape recorder, and record the introduction, which should include the date, the name of the project, the narrator's name, and the interviewer's name. Each of the three student volunteers should ask questions for five to ten minutes.

Invite the guest narrator to participate in the evaluation of the interview with the students and teacher, using the videotape of the practice interview. "Tips on How to Interview" (Handout 9) can be used as the evaluation criteria. If there's not enough time during the class, schedule the interview critique for the next day. Pause the tape at intervals and ask the students, "What follow-up question could have been asked at this point?" Involve both the student volunteers who asked the questions, and their classmates in the discussion. The students' comments are very important, and glaring mistakes often prove a valuable lesson.

■ *Project Suggestion*

Practice Interviews

Ask the students to think about the persons they will be interviewing, and how the narrator fits into the project (her age, her job, her religion—whatever is pertinent to the project). Ask the student to try to imagine what the narrator looks like, and what she might say.

Review Handouts 8 and 9, "Types of Questions to Ask" and "Tips on How to Interview," with the students, and then divide them into groups. Ask each group to come up with a skit in which they flagrantly violate some of the suggested strategies. Ask as many groups as possible to present their skits to the class. After each skit, ask the class to identify the rules that were broken. This technique, adapted from teacher-educator Paula J. Paul's "Invented" Interviews (Handout 10), invariably leads to a lot of humor and greater familiarity with interviewing strategies.

Distribute copies of "invented" interviews, or make up your own. Working in pairs, the students should read the interviews, one taking the role of interviewer, the other of narrator. Then have them reverse roles. Ask the class to evaluate these mock interviews—what worked well, what went wrong, how it could have been improved.

Equipment for the Project

There are a few practical points to consider when choosing the equipment to use for the oral history project. Although virtually all students have cassette tape recorders, it is not recommended they use their own, unless there is no alternative within your budget. Having consistency of sound reproduction is guaranteed if all the students use the same type of cassette recorder, the same type of cassettes, and the same microphones. To avoid dust and lost parts, store the equipment in a clear plastic bin with a checklist taped to the underside of the lid. Check off equipment as it is loaned out and returned.

Keep in mind that technology is rapidly changing audio recordings. Here is what you will need for a good sound recording: an inexpensive analog portable cassette tape recorder with a pause, a counter, a remote microphone outlet, new batteries, and an AC power cord. Two recording heads (this is the piece of the recorder that touches the tape) will ensure the quality of your recordings. Read the directions that come with your recorder. It is particularly important to clean the heads after about a dozen uses.

Good audio quality is necessary for using the recorded voice in public performances. It is also essential if you are asking someone to transcribe the tape. Since the internal microphones on tape recorders pick up the motor noise, quality remote microphones are a good idea, but not essential. You may want to purchase some microphones (and adapters) to loan out to students if they are using their own tape recorders. You may use either a larger, omni-directional microphone (which receives well from all directions), or two microphones, one for the narrator, one for the interviewer. (I prefer using two small lavaliere microphones that attach to the person's clothing.) A simple "Y" adapter will allow you to plug the two lines into one "microphone out" plug on the tape recorder. Digital audio tape recorders guarantee excellent quality sound and sound that can be reproduced on a computer (more about this later).

Normal bias, 60- or 90-minute cassettes are recommended. The longer the tape, the more fragile it is, meaning it is more likely to suffer from "print through" or even breakage, especially after multiple uses or during transcription. If you plan to preserve your audio recordings and to use the recordings for transcripts or public programs, it is best to make a duplicate and protect the original. This will also avoid problems if a cassette is lost. Although the Oral History Association recommends 60-minute tapes, I suggest 90-minute cassettes based on my experience. Most student-conducted interviews often take more than 60 minutes. It is an awkward interruption to change tapes in the middle of an interview, risking making a mistake like forgetting to press play/record again. It also adds to the difficulty of keeping track of each tape, to the cost of buying extra tapes and also the to the cost and time of duplicating both tapes.

If you use batteries, keep track of the hours of use. If the batteries have not been used for a long time, replace them. Batteries that run down during recording produce uneven, speeded up sound on play back or no audio at all. It is hardly worth the other costs if you do not use fresh batteries. Many microphones require batteries as well.

A note to the wise You will have spent a great deal of time preparing for the interview, hours researching and writing the questionnaire, and selecting and contacting the narrators. It is very important that the results be recorded with clear and sharp sound. A few dollars saved on purchasing the microphones or on good cassettes is wasted if the quality of the recording is poor. Studs Terkel led a panel discussion on Chicago radio entitled "It's Not the Song, It's the Singing." He meant that the sound of the narrator's voice is just as important, some would say more important, than what is being said. The 1950's project used inexpensive Sony tape recorders, but the microphone cost twice as much as the recorders. It's money worth spending, especially if the tape is going to be transcribed, used in public programs, and stored in archives or libraries for future generations. If you need to argue for the purchase of equipment, keep in mind the time investment that your students and the narrators will make to record the interviews, the cost of producing transcripts, and the cost to a library or archives of cataloguing and preserving the sound recordings.

Digital audio recording technology is readily available. Digital recordings preserve the quality of the original for further research. Although digital audio tape recorders (or DAT recorders) are expensive, the cost is likely to come down. Digital sound will revolutionize oral history projects, providing instant access to the recorded contents, and making editing for productions a classroom reality. For our 1968 oral history project we used a DAT recorder loaned to us by the university we were working with on developing the web site. We also recorded each interview with an inexpensive tape recorder as backup. The student can index or transcribe from the standard cassette. On several occasions we were grateful to have had the backup!

If you are interested in videotaping the interviews, consider a few factors along with the type of equipment: Will there be one or more cameras? Will the cameras be stationary or mobile? Will the narrator or interviewer find cameras distracting or upsetting? What will be done with the video? Will the video be edited? What is the cost of video production? Is your library or archives prepared to maintain a videotape collection? You will need a simple camcorder on a tripod, two microphones, and videotape. Many schools have the capability to edit videotape. Often the local cable television company allows the public to use the editing equipment free or at a small fee. We have videotaped our projects routinely, and used the videos for instruction and for classroom presentations. One of the project co-directors was a skilled videographer and produced a 15-minute documentary for one of the projects. Keep in mind that it takes many hours of editing time to put together a brief documentary. Again, technology is rapidly changing. Digital cameras make the cost and ease of using them well within the classroom expertise. Editing the videos and digital photographs using a computer is a relatively easy process.

The Interview

Through the oral history interviews the students and the narrators will construct a narrative of the past. It will be a story no one else has heard or read about before. It will probably be the first time this narrator will have recorded his story for the public record.

An Information Kit (Handout 11) should go with each student to the interview. It includes:

1 the narrator information form (including the address and directions for the interview),
2 the questions
3 the legal release form
4 instructions on using the equipment
5 tips reminding the student how to ask the questions
6 the equipment—an audio cassette and an extra one, fresh batteries, the tape recorder, power cord, and microphones
7 notepaper and a pencil

The interview situation can be intimidating for the first-time young adult interviewer going into a stranger's home to talk about an event the person participated in a long time ago. To help overcome the initial hesitation, the teacher might want to set up a brief pre-interview meeting between the student and narrator either at the school or in the person's home.

A plan I have used that has worked well is to have the student interviewer go with a partner on the first interview. Although only the student assigned the interview should ask the questions, just having another set of eyes and ears there is often reassuring. The partner can help set up the equipment, and remind the other about taking care of such details as signing the release form at the conclusion of the interview, and asking for photos or memorabilia. Students like this arrangement for the first interview. Since we were using a digital recorder as the primary one and an analog recorder as backup in the 1968 oral history project, it was helpful to have two students along for the interview. When it is the partner's turn to do an interview, the first interviewer goes along as the assistant.

The student is responsible for turning in the equipment and tape-recorded interview immediately after the interview (usually the next day). The teacher, or someone else, should immediately make a copy of the analog cassette and return the copy to the student who prepares the index to the cassette. The original should be labeled and filed in a folder for the narrator.

An index is indispensable to the project, especially if the interviews are not going to be transcribed. The tape is unexplored territory with no map to help you find your way. Without the index there is just an opaque 60- to 90-minute recording. The index is the map to the interview.

Using the duplicate tape and a tape recorder with a tape counter, the student indexes the tape as soon as possible after the interview, while it is still fresh in his/her mind. The student sets the counter number at 0 to begin the tape and, for each topic (i.e. set of questions on one topic), writes the counter number along with a brief description using a few key words or phrases taken directly from the recorded interview. Although tape counters are not precise, and vary from machine to machine, they do provide a point of access to the tape-recorded interviews. There may be as few as ten subjects in the index, or more than one hundred, depending on the content and the person making the index.

One of the most difficult tasks of an oral history project is to keep track of all the parts. At the start of the project, set up a file folder for each student and for each narrator. Appoint a student to be the record keeper, or take this assignment on yourself, or (best scenario) have the help of a school secretary or aide. This person's assignment is to keep the database of information for the project, either on index cards or on a computer or both (Handout 12). Here are some of the parts, which need to be tracked:

- **Potential narrators**   An entry on each person suggested for the project, including name, address, phone number, source of who suggested the person, occupation or role of significance to project. When the person is interviewed, add date of interview and name of interviewer, and any additional comments. I usually use an address database for this and a card file. The card can be given to the student to contact the narrator.
- **Schedules**   Keep a master schedule posted in the classroom or office, noting day, time and place for the interview. Mark the schedule when the interview is complete. Keeping track of who is interviewing whom is important, and you may want to have a

designated "tracker" assigned to keep the parts organized. I have asked a library aide to help me, but the teacher or a reliable student could also serve in this role.

- **Labels** Each cassette and case must be labeled with the narrator's name, the interviewer's name, the date of the interview, and the topic. Remove the plastic tab on the cassette so it cannot be taped over. Use a paper label to identify photographs or other memorabilia, and place it on the back of each photograph. Warning: do not write with a ballpoint pen on the back of a photograph.

- **Duplicating information** Duplicate the audio tape as soon as possible after the interview has been completed. Some copy services will also make duplicates of audiocassettes. If you can afford it, it is best to make two duplicates of the original cassettes and to keep one duplicate cassette for possible transcription. Return the other duplicate to the student to prepare an index to the interview (see below). Keep a record of when the duplicates were made.

- **Paper trail** Duplicate and file in the folders the following forms as the student and/or narrator returns them:
  - narrator information form
  - legal release form (discussed in Research Ethics)
  - interview index (described below)

And, if these are part of your oral history project:
  - transcript
  - narrator's story written by the student
  - notes and other written products of project
  - copies of photographs, newspaper clippings and other documents
  - copies of all correspondence between project and narrator

The student should send a thank you note with a copy of the index and, if it is possible, a duplicate tape to the narrator. The teacher and students may want to prepare a prototype thank you. If photographs have been borrowed, they should be duplicated for future use, and the originals returned. Records should be kept if the originals are to be needed for the final project or presentation. The teacher or record keeper should mail the packets to the narrators.

4

AFTER THE INTERVIEW

The oral history project should play an integral role in meeting curriculum objectives in terms of the process and/or the content. Your class should discuss and learn collaboratively throughout the project, as they brainstorm, do the background research, write the questions, conduct the interviews, and assess the results. At each step, you may want students to turn in brief, written progress reports that identify both problems and solutions. From these progress reports, you can select a few problems and solutions as case studies for directed class discussion.

In the Classroom

[handwritten:] 10 minute check-in on Tuesdays?

■ *Project Suggestion*

Debrief students in class following their interviews. Through this process students will reflect upon and share what they have learned about both interviewing and history. These are some questions that you might ask students:

- What were the highlights of your interview?
- What did you learn about the topics you covered?
- What did you learn about doing interviews?
- What were some unexpected things that happened in the interview?
- What did you learn about yourself as a result of doing the interview?
- What observations did you make during the interview about the following: body language? verbal messages?
- What would you do differently next time?

Debriefing

Paula J. Paul
Teacher Educator
Philadelphia, PA

To demonstrate the meaning and value of oral history, the interview must have an audience beyond the student interviewer, the narrator, and the teacher. As the students complete their interviews, they should prepare informal reports and class presentations about the work in progress. The report may include a brief summary of the interview content, a page-length draft transcript of a particularly revealing or significant portion of the interview, along with a selected passage from the interview to play aloud in class. If the topic of the interview assignment relates to the classroom subject matter at hand, you may key the student presentations to the class schedule. For example, interviews with veterans may be presented when the class reads about World War II, or, if several interview excerpts deal with growing up, students may present their work when the class reads a novel or short story about coming of age. The students become the class experts for a time in the subject of their own research.

You and your class will work to make sense of the interviews in context. The alternative is to give over a portion of the class to presentations and discussions around the discrete topics, themes, and patterns that emerge from the interviews. You may group and order the presentations based on information from class discussions, student progress reports, and summaries. An interview may be used in more than one discussion. Narrators, outside experts, and even school administrators may be invited to attend and comment on these informal presentations. The audience (students, teacher, and guests) should feel free to stop the playback of a recording in order to comment or ask questions. The ensuing discussion should lead students to compare and contrast the experiences and perspectives of multiple narrators. The presentations will give the students an opportunity to rehearse their final assignments.

■ *Project Suggestion*

After the Interview

Maryanne Malecki
Social Studies
Bethlehem Middle School
Delmar, NY

Eighth-grade students have interviewed friends, relatives, and neighbors regarding life experiences during the Great Depression, World War II, and the Vietnam War era. Introductory classroom lessons utilize the works of Studs Terkel taken from *The Good War* and *Hard Times*, which students read and analyze for personal, social, and historic information. In addition, as anniversaries of historic events are commemorated, students are assigned "quick interviews" of older adult individuals who were alive during the event—the assassination of John Kennedy, the D-Day invasion, the resignation of Richard Nixon—to personalize history and encourage inter-generation dialogue. Class projects have included a desktop publication of interviews of the 1930s and 1940s, immigration displays based on interviews, artifacts and documents, video and audio tapes of Vietnam reminiscence; creative writing prose and poetry based on oral histories. For a D-Day celebration, students "wore fedoras atop double-breasted zoot suits and ball gowns with long white gloves, and munched on Spam when they weren't doing the jitterbug to *In the Mood*.

Transcribing the Interview

To transcribe or not to transcribe: that is the question! The most difficult, most expensive, most time consuming, and often the most useful part of an oral history is transcribing the tape-recorded interview. An average minute of talk is equal to a double-spaced type written page of transcript. If the interview took 90 minutes, you should expect to have a 90-page transcript. Each hour of recorded interview takes 6 to 9 hours to transcribe, depending on the transcriber's skill in typing, the equipment used to transcribe, and on the clarity of the interview.

A transcript is valuable if the oral history will become a permanent part of the history of a community, region, or state and will be placed in an archive or local history collection made available to the public. The sound recording is the most complete record, providing the nuances of phrasing, emotion, dialect, and voice that are lacking in a transcript. However, since audio and videocassettes deteriorate over the years, the transcript is a more permanent record. It can also be microfilmed for storage for future generations. New digital technology may secure the longevity for print, visual, and audio recordings.

With a transcript, future generations of scholars and researchers will use and cite a common written record of information. A second benefit of a written transcript is that the narrator can read and correct errors on a transcription, providing a more accurate reporting of the events. A third benefit is its ease of use. On average, a person can read three times faster than he/she can listen. For a scholar looking for discrete information from primary sources, this can be a great advantage.

If there is money in the budget, the interview can be professionally transcribed. Without funds, community volunteers or the students may have to be the transcribers. In several of our projects, I budgeted for a professional service to transcribe the interviews. This allows us a fast return of the transcripts and a professional quality of work for the future preservation of the information.

In the "Grandma" project ninth grade students were required to transcribe their second interviews as part of the course work. They did so, but with considerable complaining, most of which was valid, given the time constraints, the difficulty, and their age. Most of their transcripts were more than 50 pages long, and this was done in the days before the computer! In the "1950's" oral history project, several students chose to transcribe their own interviews, and since there was money budgeted for that service, we were able to pay the students a fair rate, but only half what the professional service charged. The quality of the students' work in the "Fifties" project was markedly better since the students volunteered, were older, had access to computers, and were paid. The advent of computer word processors has made transcribing much easier. In the "1968" oral history project the students transcribed their first interviews. We rented two transcribing machines which made the job much easier, but the scheduling more difficult.

Lessons learned from these experiences are numerous:

- students can do an adequate, even admirable job transcribing their interviews;
- forcing students to invest the hours in transcribing is questionable as a vehicle for learning;
- students who transcribe may increase their language, word processing, and listening skills
- students will know the narrator better than anyone else

Here are two-low budget strategies:

1 Require students to write indexes of the tape content and then transcribe the most significant portions. (Note the transcribed portions on the index.)
2 Use teams to record and transcribe the interviews, dividing the work among a few students. As you plan this part of the process, keep in mind that transcripts, indexes, and other written records must be saved in a standardized word processing format for future publication and use.

■ *Project Suggestion*

Turning the Lens on Oneself

Robert J. Allison
Claire S. Schen
Suffolk University
Boston, MA

Students tend not to think of history as a participatory event. For the most part, history happens to other people. They are uncertain if their own memories constitute an "interesting" topic, despite the connection of memory to family, custom, and origins. This exercise opens a new line of inquiry, encouraging students to reflect upon themselves and others as "historical actors." In this assignment, students discuss their own history and culture. The students are paired, and each partner asks a series of questions about culture and family history. Their reports are used to trace the history of twentieth century immigration to America. Suffolk students offer unique opportunities for this. About half of the students are third- or fourth-generation Americans, of Irish or Italian or Chinese ancestry. The rest are either international students, studying in the United States before returning to their native country, or are immigrants themselves. Students learn how their own history is part of the larger fabric of social history. Students and their partners make oral presentations about culture, community, self, and family history. Teachers synthesize the contents of presentations and make connections to historical trends and themes.

Since there is not enough time to transcribe, consider using just the tape-recorded interview and its index to gather whatever information is needed. Other possibilities are: a page-long written summary of the information on the tape, along with a one-page analysis and interpretation of the information; an abridged transcript (described above); a larger research paper using quotes and information from the interview; an edited version of the audiotape; or an oral report on the subject using several minutes of the narrator's comments which could be enhanced with photographs, a photograph collage, or slides.

You may also produce a public forum to share your results and to discuss the issues raised in the project. Participants could include students, narrators, and/or experts in the subject area. A public forum is a good way to inform the community of what has been going on in the classroom, and to educate the public about the topic itself. Have the students help with the publicity for the event by creating a flyer, making public announcements, and writing a press release.

A longer (more than 4 weeks) project

If the students are assigned only one interview, there will be time to transcribe, if a transcript is important to the project. Here are some possible assignments:

- **Interview transcript**   Using a word processor, and following a pre-established format, the student transcribes his or her own interview. The assignment is evaluated on the quality of the transcript (how many grammatical errors, spelling errors, and inaccuracies) and on its completeness. Using an established format ensures that a library or archives can catalog the transcripts consistently. The disk should become part of the permanent record, along with a backup in case the original is lost or damaged. The teacher should read the transcripts and work with the students to determine the historically significant aspects of the narrators' interviews.

The transcripts can be used in all of the following assignments:

- **A written report**   Using the transcript of the interview, notes from guest speakers, and the research conducted on the context of the topic, the student writes a report, quoting and paraphrasing the narrator to support the thesis.
- **An oral report**   The student explains and interprets the narrator's story to the class. The student must be ready to defend and support any hypothesis or statement made in the report.

- **A dramatic performance** The student assumes the role of the narrator, and using the narrator's words relates an eyewitness moment of history in a kind of "You Are There" performance. Or the student, either alone or with a partner, writes a script using direct dialogue from the transcript and stages a dramatic performance.

- **First person or autobiographical narrative** Students seem to be comfortable taking on the *persona* of the person they interviewed. They first identify the parts of the interview that are historically significant. Next the student outlines the narrator's story. Although most students like to "begin at the beginning" with the person's birth, they should be encouraged to write the story from the most dramatic aspects of the interview and then flash backwards or forwards as the story progresses. In other words, tell a good story, using verbatim quotes from the transcript, omitting the questions asked and irrelevant material. The student must not invent or create material or describe situations as the student might imagine them. The student is *not* creating a work of fiction.

- **Question and answer format** The student may choose to write the narrator's story in an interview style, inserting himself as the person asking the questions. The narrator's responses and sometimes the student's analysis of the responses form the content of the story. The student chooses the significant aspects of the interview to focus on, and quotes directly from the transcript.

■ *Project Suggestion*

Women and Work

Gail J. Sklar
Simon Gratz High School
Philadelphia, PA

The students explored the question "Why is gender valued more than skill?" in a study of women in the work force. For the assignment, students researched, using at least three books and other information. Students described how women work harder than men do and where this problem originated. Their research covered family life, gender roles, and social organization. The project results included oral histories, a research bibliography, a written personal reflection, and a creative piece such as a dance, a one-scene play, or a board game.

Lisa Rowland
Middletown Senior High
School, Middletown, OH

Social studies and English teachers at Middletown High School collaborated on a study of women's work. Students learned about doing oral history and studied the role of women in history and the economy before conducting interviews with women of various ages and occupations about their education, their work, and their expectations regarding work and family lives. Students wrote, edited, and published summaries of these interviews on the Internet. The teachers concluded the project with a multimedia production that summed up the project for their classes, and held a public reception, inviting the school board.

You and the students have completed the research, formulated the questions, interviewed narrators, collected original historical documentation, indexed and transcribed the interviews. What do you do with this "gold mine" of local history? Here are a few suggestions, but I'm sure you will have your own ideas.

- **Audio documentary** Technically challenging, a radio documentary can provide one of the most accessible project outcomes. This is a common use of oral history on public radio. While radio documentaries were made long before digital recordings were available, digital (DAT) recording permits mixing and editing the sound on a computer. A local radio station may be willing to help with this project and may air the documentary. If the school system has the technical capability, this could be a wonderful use of oral history material. The student edits the narrator's voice from the recorded interview to focus on the most interesting and dramatic stories told and records an introduction or an audio essay that incorporates interview segments. *Note* Transcripts make the editing job far easier.

- **Video documentary** Also technically challenging, a video will provide even greater accessibility than radio. Most cable television stations are required to cablecast public access TV programs. Many schools have video-editing equipment. Preparing a 20- to 30-minute production is an exciting way to present the information to the public. Like the radio script, the students use the transcript to select the most dramatic stories. In addition to the video of the narrator talking, the student (or audiovisual specialist) may insert photographs and video footage depicting some of the subjects, as well as copyright-free music and voice-over narration.

- **Slide/tape presentation or a PowerPoint-type presentation** This production includes aspects of both sound and picture. It can incorporate the recorded voices of the narrators, photographs, slides, drawings and portraits depicting the events. For "The Wake of '38" oral history project, conducted before digital technology, the students and teachers created slides and used the audio from the interviews to depict the series of events of the great hurricane of September 21, 1938. Music, narration and dialogue were combined with archival photographs and amateur snapshots. Computer presentation software can enhance the slide/tape presentation and allow you to integrate sound more precisely.

- **Exhibit** If the students have gathered and duplicated photographs, newspaper articles, and other documents, or if they have taken photographs of the narrators during the project, your students can produce an exhibit. Brief excerpts from the transcripts make excellent captions for an exhibit that can be set up in the school, a public library, or a city building. For an exhibit, consider using the National History Day standards and assigning students individually or in small teams their own sections to design and produce.

- **Tour** If you have studied the community or a neighborhood, the students can either lead or record a tour of a local building, neighborhood, park or other site, using passages from oral history interviews to enliven the local history. The students could write and publish a "walking tour" or "guided tour" pamphlet with photographs and quotations from the narrators' stories.

- **Performance** You may be able to work with your students to produce a play based on the many narratives in the interviews. Since the interviews are spoken words, the words and phrases often lend themselves to such a production.

- **World Wide Web** This is perhaps the most exciting application of oral history to come about since video. The technology is available in many schools to produce an interactive multi-media program, or to create a site on the World Wide Web, combining sound from the tape-recorded interviews, photographs, film and video footage, print and historical documentation. The combination of these sound, visual, and print components with the written word and with links to related Internet resources is the perfect medium to present local history to the public. For an example, look at the Web site for "1968: The Whole World Was Watching" at http://www.stg.brown.edu/projects/1968/.

You may want to combine different forms of production. In any case, a public program is an appropriate outcome for an oral history project and an excellent opportunity for your students to earn recognition for their hard work. Remember to invite the project narrators, school administrators, other public figures, and the local press to a reception when you launch your public program.

When the oral history project is complete, place the original audiocassettes, the release forms, the information form, the index, the transcripts, collected memorabilia, and the students' final presentations or products in a safe and secure location. In many states there is an archive for oral history collections. Check with the state historical society or a university for the most suitable place to determine the best location in your community or state to permanently store and catalog the original documentation and related information. The Special Collections Department of the University of Rhode Island library is our state oral history archive. If funds allow, you may want to give copies of the documentation to both a local repository and to the state historical society. Inform the public, through a press release, that the information is available.

Preserving the Historical Documents

■ *Project Suggestion*

The focus of the work at the Bland County History Archives is recording the oral histories of this area of Appalachia. The students maintain the archives. They consist of over 200 oral history interviews, cemetery catalogues, hundreds of photographs, maps, and artifacts. The collection is housed in the former Honaker Church building, which is the oldest extant building in Rocky Gap. The holdings are continuously being added to. The goal of the archives is "to preserve the stories of the people and Bland County and present them to the public in a variety of ways. Many of the stories are the stories of the last people to have been born and raised in a real log cabin back up a holler or on top of a mountain. These are the unique stories of Appalachia as told by its people. (http://bland.k12.va.us/bland/rocky/links.html)

The Bland County History Archives

Rocky Gap High School
Rocky Gap, VA

There are several ways to work student assessment into the oral history project, depending on the length and scope of the project. Students should be told at the start how they will be evaluated. In the projects I co-taught with the English teacher, we evaluated both the content and the process. The teacher was responsible for the content, quizzing the students on their reading assignments, checking on their listening skills when guest speakers were invited, and grading the writing assignments. As the oral historian, I evaluated the students' skills in researching the topic, learning interview techniques, preparing the index (and sometimes the transcript) of the tape, and selecting significant parts of the interview to include in the written story. Together the teacher and I evaluated how well the students handled each aspect of the process: setting up and conducting the interview, getting the correct forms filled out and returned, labeling the material, meeting the deadlines, and finally, the student's conduct and responsibility throughout the oral history project (Handout 14).

Assessment and Student Evaluation

The students can be involved in the assessment of their work and the evaluation of the oral history project (Handout 13). Their participation, enthusiasm, and willingness to do more than what is required will indicate the success of the project. In every oral history project we have taught most students have exceeded the requirements for the semester's work. Even after the conclusion of the oral history project and the course it was part of, the students have been eager to stay involved. Our projects have had a public forum component to meet the state humanities council guidelines. The students have taken active roles in these forums, which were held evenings and Saturdays, and often during the following semester or school year. The students helped write press releases, designed the flyers and made sure the persons they interviewed attended. Several students volunteered to speak at the forums, or to lead the discussions. It's a terrific opportunity for the school to show the community what's going on in education.

Students who were sophomores in the class that conducted the "1950's" asked for copies of the publication two years later when they were applying to colleges. "I'm a published author," wrote a student in her college essay, and proceeded to describe her role in the oral history.

A classroom oral history project contains all the components of a good education. First, it actively engages the students in a classroom activity that is relevant and significant. Second, students are shown how different aspects of the curriculum are interrelated, that is, how learning in one classroom can relate to learning in another classroom. Third, students learn that the process of learning is as important as the content learned. Fourth, students learn that education can take place outside the classroom. Fifth, the students learn communication skills that are applicable to life situations. Finally, the product of the students' oral history project becomes an historical document in itself, an important resource for the community, and in some cases for the state, country, and even world.

One of the most important lessons the student learns is that individuals are part of the greater society, and that the individual is shaped by society and in turn helps to shape society. The students get a snapshot of another person's life as it interacts with events outside that life. They learn how the individual reacts to the events, learns from them, and attempts to exert control over them. In every interview in every oral history project, the narrators explain what they saw, what they did, and what they thought about the things that they were experiencing. The students listen and learn from these interviews. They learn that history is assembled from these human pieces, that no one piece is any less important than any other piece, and that they have a role in making sure the pieces are not lost.

An oral history is not just the song, but it is also the singing. Each human life is a brief historical note, which becomes part of the song of life. If a recording is made of the notes, then the future can listen and learn. The value to historians and scholars, which include our young students, is to find the answers to the question *why? Why then and not now? Why here and not there? Why me and not you?* These are the puzzling pieces of history. A classroom oral history project will suggest answers for the future by preserving the pieces of the past.

Allen, Barbara and Lynwood Montell. *From Memory to History: Using Oral Sources in Local Historical Research.* Nashville: American Association for State and Local History, 1981.

Baum, Willa K. *Oral History for the Local Historical Society.* Revised Edition. Nashville: American Association for State and Local History, 1987.

_____. *Transcribing and Editing Oral History.* Nashville: American Association for State and Local History, 1977.

Brecher, Jeremy. *History from Below: How to Uncover and Tell the Story of Your Community, Association, or Union.* New Haven, CT: Commonwork Pamphlets/Advocate Press, 1986.

Brown, Cynthia Stokes. *Like It Was: A Complete Guide to Writing Oral History.* Teachers and Writers Collaborative. (ISBN 0-914924-12-9)

Dean, Pamela, Toby Daspit, and Petra Munro. *Talking Gumbo: a Teacher's Guide to Using Oral History in the Classroom.* (Companion video: *You've Got to Hear This Story*) Louisiana State University: T. Harry Williams Center, 1998.

Dunaway, David K. and Willa K. Baum. *Oral History: An Interdisciplinary Anthology.* Nashville: American Association for State and Local History, 1984.

Eff, Elaine. *You Should Have Been Here Yesterday.* Maryland Historical Trust, 1995. (Contact 1 (800) 756-0119 or vanwie@dhcd.state.md.us)

Fletcher, William P. *Recording Your Family History: A Guide to Preserving Oral History with Videotape, Audio Tape, Suggested Topics and Questions, Interview Techniques.* New York: Dodd, Mead & Co., 1986, 1989.

Frank, Benjamin M. *A "Do-It-Yourself" Oral History Primer.* Marine Corps Oral History Program, Marine Corps Historical Center, Building 50, Washington Navy Yard, 901 M Street SE, Washington, DC 20374.

Frisch, Michael. *A Shared Authority: Essays on the Craft and Meaning of Oral and Public History.* Albany: State University of New York Press, 1990.

Grele, Ronald J., ed. *Envelopes of Sound: The Art of Oral History*. Revised Edition. Westport, CT: Meckler, 1990.

Hamer, Lynne. "Oralized History: History Teachers as Oral History Tellers," *The Oral History Review*. Summer/Fall 2000, Vol. 27, No. 2.

Hickey, M. Gail. *Bringing History Home: Local and Family History Projects for Grades K–6*. Boston: Allyn and Bacon, 1999.

History from the Living: The Organization and Craft of Oral History, based on "1968: The Whole World Was Watching" oral history project, South Kingstown High School, Wakefield, RI. Newport, RI: Grin Productions, 1998. Running time 17 minutes 14 seconds. Companion video to *Oral History Projects in Your Classroom*. Available from J. Long, Grin Productions, 6 Carey Street, Newport, RI 02804, $20.

H-Oralhist, affiliated with the Oral History Association, is an H-Net network for scholars and professionals active in studies related to oral history. The address is H-ORALHIST@H-NET.MSU.EDU. The web site is http://www.h-net.msu.edu/~oralhist/.

Ives, Edward D. *An Oral Historian's Work*. Oral History Instructional Videotape. Blue Hills Falls, ME 04615: Northeast Historic Film, 1988.

_____. *The Tape Recorded Interview: A Manual for Field Workers in Folklore and Oral History*. Knoxville: University of Tennessee Press, 1995.

Jolly, Brad. *Videotaping Local History*. Nashville: American Association for State and Local History, 1982.

Kuhn, Cliff and Marjorie L. McLellan, eds. *Magazine of History,* Oral History special issue, June 1996.

Lanman, Barry. *The Promised Land: The Discovery Learning Community Teachers and Learners Guide Support for Oral History*. http://school.discovery.com/learningcomm/promisedland/teachandlearn/oralguide/.

Lee, Charles R. and Kathryn L. Nasstrom, eds. "Practice and Pedagogy: Oral History in the Classroom," Special issue of *The Oral History Review* 25/1–2 (Summer/Fall 1998).

McLellan, Marjorie L. *Oral History Resources for Teachers: Miami Valley Cultural Heritage Project*. http://www.muohio.edu/oralhistory.eduction.htm.

McMahan, Eva M. and Kim Lacy Rogers, eds. *Interactive Oral History Interviewing*. Lea's Communication, 1994.

Mercier, Laurie and Madeline Buckendorf. *Using Oral History in Community History Projects*. Los Angeles: Oral History Association, Pamphlet No. 4, 1992.

Neuenschwander, John N. *Oral History and the Law*. Second Edition. Los Angeles: Oral History Association, Pamphlet No. 1, 1993.

The Oral History Association promotes the teaching and practice of oral history internationally through the quarterly newsletter *Oral History Review,* an annual conference, and a variety of publications. Oral History Association, Dickinson College, P. O. Box 1773, Carlisle, PA 17013-2896. E-mail to oha@dickinson.edu. The web site for the Oral History Association is http://www.dickinson.edu/oha.

Oral History Evaluation Guidelines. Second Edition. Los Angeles: Oral History Association, Pamphlet No. 3, 1991. Also available on the OHA website (see above).

Perks, Robert and Alistair Thomson. *The Oral History Reader*. New York and London: Routledge, 1998.

Ritchie, Donald A. *Doing Oral History*. New York: Twayne Publishers, 1995.

Rosenzweig, Roy and David Thelen. *The Presence of the Past: Popular Uses of History in American Life*. New York: Columbia University Press, 1998.

Stearns, Peter Yuen. *Meaning Over Memory: Recasting the Teaching of Culture and History*. Chapel Hill: University of North Carolina Press, 1993.

Stricklin, David and Rebecca Sharpless, eds. *The Past Meets the Present: Essays on Oral History*. Lanham, MD: University Press of America, 1988.

Sturdevant, Katherine Scott. *Bringing Your Family History to Life Through Social History*. Cincinnati: Betterway Books, 2000.

Thompson, Paul. *Oral History: The Voice of the Past*. Revised Edition. New York: Oxford University Press, 1988.

The following excerpt is from a student interview with John Sullivan, a Democratic Party leader from Dayton, Ohio. In this excerpt, "Sully" describes the scene at the 1968 Democratic Party National Convention in Chicago. Before you discuss the interview passage, write down a few questions about the events, the accuracy of the description, and the narrator's point of view. After reading and discussing their questions about the passage, ask students what questions they would like to have asked. Discuss how the scene might be described differently from the perspective of the Ohio college students, the "agitators," or "Mayor Daley's cops." Ask your students to assess the strengths and weakness of this interview as an historical document.

Interviews and Transcripts as Primary Sources

Interview with John Sullivan, Dayton, OH, by Shaun Stevens

Instructor
Dr. Marjorie L. McLellan
Miami University
Middletown, OH

The next real convention was in '68, which was the riot convention. That was a horrible experience. We got there and checked in to our hotel. Well, it just so happens that there was trouble coming so all the help had just conveniently not shown up. So what they did was they hired the old timers that had been there-you know, for a hundred years, out of the rest homes. The first thing I knew we had trouble because I saw the clerk-she was about ninety-and all these people [were] yelling for their keys. Finally she got so mad at them, she threw the first number of keys to us. Naturally, it wasn't our room. So finally we got the house detective to open our room on the seventh floor—Shannahan was his name, big feet and I knew that he was going to be our doorkeeper for a long time. I knew that we would see him maybe once, that was the end of Shannahan.

That was about right. So we couldn't lock our door, and they didn't have any room service. We had four politicians in there all smoking cigars and drinking coffee and having meetings. . . . It looked like a refuse dump after the first two days. And the hippy-dippies were running around quite a bit. So you go to a restaurant, for example, you sit down to eat your chow, and all of a sudden it would be like a whale of hippy-dippies come by-girls and guys-mostly college age. They would go up to your food and say, "Can I have a little piece?" and they would hack off a little chunk of your hamburger or something and go on their way. [They would] say, "Thank you." Then at nighttime when you get back, for the first seven floors of the hotel are full of hippy-dippies sleeping on the floors, in the hallways. And in the morning you hear a little knock on the door and a couple of hippy-dippies out there [saying], "Can we use your bathroom? So, naturally we didn't have any keys, so we let the suckers in.

Then at two o'clock when we got back to our hotel, we'd have a staff meeting. Ohio was bracketed with California, so we would have all these hippy-dippies and these highly-educated intellectuals, you know, and we'd be having our meeting of what we were going to do tomorrow, and it's three o'clock in the morning. Well, infiltrated in our group was always some of Mayor Daley's cops. And they were so subtle: (you know the temperature was about a hundred and ninety in Chicago) They had to have suits on and burr haircuts. (Sullivan laughs). And they sit together. So the pretty little girls there would try to get them drunk or give them marijuana cookies and a few times they were successful and they would arrest us all. But, anyway, that was the way the convention was- it was terrible.

And they had tear-gas all over the place, and every morning, it's like we in Ohio, we'd come and bring our brightest children with us-college kids from Miami [University] and UD [University of Dayton], all the wonderful schools, you know. They'd have their school shirts on. And they say good-bye to Mama, like Mama would be a commissioner or a mayor, and they go up to the Conrad Hilton Hotel, as I recall, and there's a park across the street to meet the people. What the dummies didn't know [was that] they were going to be used as fronts. See, they had all these nice, little clean-cut and well-scrubbed kids from different cities, and countries, for that matter, and you had nuns and Red Cross people. They were in the front lines. But in the back lines were all these forty-year-old students who were running the whole agitation. Right about 8:30, they start throwing rocks. Well, the cops had been there, they got tired of that, see . . .. And then the little National Guard, they like to shoot anybody, anyway. So after about three or four rock throwing times, about 9:30 every morning, the cops would charge. And anybody in the front row would get knocked down: the nuns, the reporters, the Red Cross, and the kids.

Complete the sentence and then answer the follow-up questions below.

Witness to History

Ora Cooks
School of Education
Clark Atlanta University

"I believe I was a witness to history because I was there when
(what happened?)

_____ . "

1 What role did you play in this event?

2 How did you feel about what happened?

3 Who else was there and what did the person(s) do?

4 Where did this happen?

5 When did this happen?

6 What do you believe caused this to happen?

7 What were the effects/results of the event?

8 How do you feel about the event now?

Use school letterhead.

Date _____

Name _____

Phone Number _____

Address _____

Date of birth _____

Present occupation _____

Occupation during time we are researching _____

Briefly describe what your experience focused on during the time period we are researching.

_____

_____

Where were you living then? _____

Where would you prefer to be interviewed? ❏ Home ❏ Office ❏ School

Can you suggest someone else to be interviewed? Please give name, address and phone number, or how we might reach the person.

_____

_____

Return to *(fill in school address)* _____

Interview scheduled for *(date, time, place)* _____

Student interviewer _____

Use school letterhead.

Dear

Thank you for being willing to share your memories and experiences of the year 1968, the climatic year of the turbulent 1960s. Our project, "1968: The Whole World Was Watching" is a classroom oral history project sponsored by the South Kingstown School Department and the Rhode Island Historical Society. The Rhode Island Committee for the Humanities has funded the project.

The students will interview approximately 30 persons from all aspects of Rhode Island life, and ask them to reflect on the major themes of 1968—the Vietnam War, politics, popular culture, civil rights and women's issues.

Students will write the narrators' stories for a publication that will be distributed by the Rhode Island Historical Society. The narrators' stories will also become part of an Internet Web Site, designed by the Scholarly Technology Group at Brown University. Photographs of the narrators and historical photographs will be collected. Two public forums in the fall of 1998 will be held to present the project to the public.

The students will not be able to interview everyone who has contacted us, or whom we have contacted. Please complete and return the enclosed information form to have your name added to the pool of narrators from which we will select the persons to be interviewed. Age, experience, and relation to the theme and events of the period will determine selection of the narrators. Those chosen will be asked to sign a Release Form which gives permission to the South Kingstown High School and the Rhode Island Historical Society to use the information in the recorded interview for any educational and historical purposes they deem appropriate.

If you are chosen, a student will contact you at the end of March to make an appointment with you for the interview. If you have any questions about the project, contact *(project director)*.

Please complete and return the enclosed Information Form. We look forward to hearing from you. Thank you very much.

First, find two dates that will work for you and for availability of tape recorder, partner, etc. Is transportation necessary?

Narrator's name and phone number _____

SPEAK SLOOOOWWWWWLY . . .

Hello, I'm *(your name)*_____ from *(name of school)*_____.
I will be interviewing you about your memories and experiences of *(topic/ period being researched)*_____.

I would like to set up a day, time and place for the interview. We will need about two hours of time. Would *(suggest day and time)*_____ be a good day and time for you? Could we choose a second date just in case the first one isn't good for my partner? I will call you back to confirm the date. *(If interview will be at narrator's home or office ask for directions.)* If there is a problem you can call me at *(your phone number)* _____.

Thank you very much. I'm looking forward to interviewing you.

Second date _____

Directions _____

_____

_____

_____

_____

_____

_____

Use school letterhead. Make one copy for the lender and one copy for the borrower.

Name of Narrator/Lender _____

Address _____

Phone Number _____

Name of Interviewer/Borrower _____

Address _____

Phone Number _____

Materials borrowed _____

_____

_____

Conditions for use _____

_____

_____

Date when material should be returned _____

Signature of Lender _____

                                       Date _____

Signature of Borrower _____

                                       Date _____

Use school letterhead.

I have tape recorded an interview for South Kingstown High School in conjunction with the Rhode Island Historical Society and the Scholarly Technology Group at Brown University, and set forth my observations, memories and experiences surrounding the events and issues of the year 1968.

I hearby give and grant to South Kingstown High School, the Rhode Island Historical Society, and the Scholarly Technology Group, or anyone authorized by them, the absolute and unqualified right to the use of this tape recorded interview for such scholarly and educational purposes as they shall determine.

It is expressly understood that the full literary rights of this interview pass to South Kingstown High School, the Rhode Island Historical Society, and the Scholarly Technology Group, and that no rights whatsoever are to vest in my heirs now or at my death.

I hearby release and discharge the South Kingstown High School, the Rhode Island Historical Society, and the Scholarly Technology Group from any and all claims and demands arising out of, or in connection with, the use of such observations, memories and experiences of 1968, including, but not limited to, any and all claims of libel, slander, and invasion of privacy.

I understand this does not preclude any use I would want to make of the material therein.

Narrator name and address *(please print)* _____

_____

Signature _____ Date _____

Interviewer name and address *(please print)* _____

_____

Signature _____ Date _____

To be a good interviewer, you need to

- be a good listener!
- be curious!

There are two kinds of questions:

- open
- closed

Except to pinpoint a specific date or time, name of person, or identify an event, all your questions should be open-ended.

Many of your questions will ask *why: Why wouldn't the crowd leave?*

Some questions ask *how: How did his death affect you?*

Some questions will be *suggestive: You said you were taking a class at the university. Could you tell me more about it?*

Suggestive questions also ask the narrator to *reflect in more detail* on an experience: *What else do you think the Weather Bureau could have done to warn people about the hurricane?*

Some questions will be *descriptive: Could you describe the size of the crowd? Could you describe your injury?*

Here's a question that asks for a *definition: Would you explain what "spooling" means in your work?*

Some questions need a *follow-up: Could you tell me more about your experiences as a rescue helicopter pilot?*

One of the hardest kinds of question to ask is the *negative question: Many people felt the war protesters were unpatriotic. What were your feelings?*

When you are dealing with sensitive issues (drugs, sex, crime), allow the narrator to respond in the *third person: There was a lot of drug use during this time, especially LSD and marijuana. Were you aware of any of your friends who were using these drugs? What were some of their experiences like?*

1   Listen. An interview is not a dialogue. The whole point is to get the narrator to tell his/her story. Listen for clues and leads. Be alert and ready to follow up.

2   Be curious. Ask the narrator to explain things to you; define words and phrases you're not familiar with; describe physical things.

3   Ask one question at a time. If the narrator hears a string of questions, he/she usually only answers the first or the last question.

4   Smile and nod your head. Look at the narrator and encourage him with your eyes and body. If he thinks he is boring you, he'll stop talking.

5   Silence can be golden. Give your narrator a chance to think of what she wants to say. Keep quiet and wait; count to ten slowly before asking another question or repeating the question. Relax and write a few words on your note pad.

6   Do not interrupt a good story. But, if he digresses guide him back to the topic as politely as you can. You might say, "That's very interesting, but I'd like you to talk about . . .."

7   Do not challenge or contradict the narrator. The interview is not an interrogation. You are just collecting as much information as possible that can be used.

8   Try to avoid off-the-record information. Ask him to let you record the whole thing and promise him he can edit or have it erased later.

9   End the interview at a reasonable time (usually 60 to 90 minutes). Always ask if there is anything else she would like to talk about or go back to. Pause before thanking her and turning the recorder off.

10 Thank the narrator and have him/her sign the release form.

Tips on How to Interview

None of these interview situations are real, but they demonstrate certain "right" and "wrong" ways to interview. Workings with groups of two, ask each student to read a part. Have them discuss with his/her partner what "interview tips" have been broken and what "tips" have been successful in each situation. Switch roles between examples.

"Invented" Interviews for Practice

Credit for the idea to Paula Paul Oral historian and teacher Philadelphia, PA

Interview Situation 1

I Do you remember when you learned of Martin Luther King's death? Could you describe how you felt and what you did or said?

N I was downstairs writing a paper for my college English class when my upstairs neighbor came running down the stairs telling me the news. We both turned on the television to learn about it.

I What did you see?

N We watched NBC and they reported that he had been shot on a balcony in Nashville, Tennessee.

I Was it Nashville or Memphis?

N It was Memphis, right! We saw interviews with the police and with King's friends. They played parts of his speech the night before when he said he wasn't afraid of death.

I What were you thinking at the time?

Interview Situation 2

I Who killed Robert Kennedy?

N Someone named Sirhan

I Did you see the murder?

N No, but I saw pictures on television and in the news the next day.

I Oh. You didn't see it then?

N No, but I can remember when I heard about it.

I Did they catch the guy?

Interview Situation 3

I There was a lot of racism in America in the sixties. Did you see much of it in your hometown?

N No, there was no racism here.

I What about other places?

N I wouldn't know.

I Did you see any scenes of racism on television?

N No.

I What were your feelings when you learned of Martin Luther King's assassination?

N I don't remember

Interview Situation 4

I You have said you participated in a lot of protests and demonstrations when you were young. What was the reaction of your parents?

N They were very negative. They felt America was right. That people who burned the flag were wrong. They felt the U.S. should be in Vietnam, and that people who went to Canada to escape the draft were wrong.

I What was your favorite song?

N I liked anything Peter, Paul and Mary sang, or Joan Baez.

I What was your favorite movie?

N I saw *The Graduate* five times!

I Do you remember when Lyndon Johnson said he would not run?

N Oh, yes.

I Where were you when you heard Martin Luther King was assassinated?

1   Set up the interview. Check the master schedule for a couple of available dates for the interview. Call the narrator and introduce yourself (see Handout 5). Write your name on the Master Schedule for date and time of confirmed interview. Notify the photographer, of date, time, and place of interview. Arrange for transportation.

2   Review the Information Form for your narrator. Become very familiar with the questions before you go to the interview. Should you add some questions? Delete some? Think about who you are interviewing and what unique experiences he/she might have to share. If you feel uncomfortable do some additional research.

3   Checklist for interview:
    ❏ label tape
    ❏ tape recorder(s)
    ❏ microphones
    ❏ backup tapes
    ❏ questionnaire
    ❏ pencil and note pad
    ❏ release form
    ❏ receipt for borrowed documents
    ❏ manila envelope with narrator's name for items

4   Arrive promptly and introduce yourself. Set up the equipment where both of you will be comfortable. Be aware of any possible interruptions or outside noise. Explain that you will be asking many questions and there is lots of time to respond. Tell narrator you will be asking her to sign a release form at the end of the interview.

5   Check the equipment. Be sure everything is working. Get pencil and note pad and questionnaire out. Put tape into recorder. Load backup recorder, if using one.

6   Hold *record* and press *pause*. When ready, release pause and give the date, the project name, your name and the name of the narrator. Press pause again.

Information Kit

Checklist for the Interview

7 Everything in order? Both of you ready? Release pause by pressing pause again. Solid red light will show you are recording. Relax, smile, give lots of positive non-verbal feedback. Remember your "tips" on how to ask questions.

8 Keep your mind focused on the interview and what is being said. Follow up leads.

9 Press pause (not stop) if there is an interruption. Red light will blink.

10 When recorder clicks off at end of side one of the tape, turn the tape over, press play and record, wait a few seconds, and continue. Red light will be solid when recording!

11 At end of recording session, give the narrator the Release Form, and collect the equipment while the narrator signs.

Keeping Track of the Parts

Student	Thank you	Photo, etc.	Release	Backup	Tape	Info Form	Narrator

Narrator	Info Form	Tape	Backup	Release	Photo, etc.	Thank you	Student

1 Do you feel you had sufficient background
  to conduct your interviews?   Yes   No   **Student Survey**
  Comment   **Evaluation**

2 Did you receive sufficient training for using
  the recording equipment?   Yes   No
  Comment

3 Do you feel the speakers were valuable?   Yes   No
  Comment

4 Do you feel you were sufficiently informed
  about how to do oral history?   Yes   No
  Comment

5 Do you feel the curriculum reflected
  the themes of the project?   Yes   No
  Comment

6 Were there any surprising outcomes for
  you from the oral history project?   Yes   No
  Comment

7 Do you feel the oral history project was a
  valuable learning experience?   Yes   No
  Comment

8 What did you enjoy most? Least?
  Comment

Student Name _____   **Project Evaluation Form**

Narrator Name _____

Points Possible

- Interview completed   20
  - on time   5
  - quality   5

- Transcript completed   20
  - on time   5
  - quality   5

- Final Project completed   20
  - on time   5
  - quality   5

- Student Conduct   10

  Total Points   *100*

Points Assigned

- Interview completed   _____
  - on time   _____
  - quality   _____

- Transcript completed   _____
  - on time   _____
  - quality   _____

- Final Project completed   _____
  - on time   _____
  - quality   _____

- Student Conduct   _____

  Total Points   _____

CPSIA information can be obtained
at www.ICGtesting.com
Printed in the USA
BVHW061616280121
598864BV00013B/969